Teens & Young People Who Impacted the World

From Modern Times to Ancient Times

Wayne Perryman

Book Publishers Network

Book Publishers Network
P.O. Box 2256
Bothell • WA • 98041
Ph • 425-483-3040
www.bookpublishersnetwork.com

Copyright © 2013 by Wayne Perryman
P.O. Box 256
Mercer Island, WA 98040
doublebro@aol.com

All rights reserved. No part of this book may be reproduced, stored in, or introduced into a retrieval system, or transmitted in any form, or by any means (electronic, mechanical, photocopying, recording, or otherwise) without the prior written permission of the publisher.

10 9 8 7 6 5 4 3 2 1

Printed in the United States of America

LCCN   2012949544
ISBN   978-1-937454-56-2

Editor: Kathy Bradley
Cover Designer: Wayne Perryman
Interior Designer: Stephanie Martindale

"*...I have written you young men, because you are strong....*" I John 2:14

"*...Your young shall see visions....*" Joel 2:28

This book is dedicated to America's talented teenagers and to those teens who may feel isolated, insignificant, hopeless, dejected and disrespected and may have given up on life.

And to:

Ms. Brookins and Dr. Wendell Smith, my heart beats because of them.

Contents

Introduction	vii
Oprah Winfrey	1
Bill Gates	9
Rosa Parks & Young Claudette Colvin	15
The Teens & Dr. King	21
Teenagers: America's Young Warriors	37
Albert Einstein	41
Jan Matzeliger	47
Thomas Edison	51
Dr. George Washington Carver	57
Florence Nightingale	65
Wolfgang Amadeus Mozart	71
Leonardo da Vinci	75
Mother Teresa	79
Jesus Inspiring Good in Others	85
Mary – Jesus's Teenage Mother	91
Advice to Young Women	95
Advice for Young Men	97
APPENDIX I: Court's Decision in Browder *vs* Gayle	99
APPENDIX II: Dr. King & The Democratic Governors of Jim Crow	101

Teens and Young People Who Impacted the World

APPENDIX III: Scripture References of Jesus,
    Mary & Young Jewish Leaders
        Jesus Early Life   119
        Mary the Teenage Mother of Jesus   123
        Jesus's Teenage Disciples   125
Bibliography   141

Introduction

There has always been a false assumption that much of the technology and many of the inventions and social improvements that we enjoy today were produced and/or developed by adult men and women. Perhaps this assumption took root when someone coined the phrase: "Children should be seen and not heard." The problem with this saying, is that it discounts and undermines the intelligence of all children and ignores their contributions to the world at large, particularly in the areas of religion, science, and social justice.

This book highlights the works of many renowned persons like the following, who started pursuing their career interests as a child i.e. Bill Gates, age 13; Oprah Winfrey, age 3; Mother Teresa, age 12; Mozart, age 5; Florence Nightingale, age 16; Albert Einstein, age 12; Dr. George Washington Carver, age 5; Leonardo Da Vinci, age 15; and Thomas Edison, age 12 to name a few.

While reading the biographies of these historical figures, you will note their parents' actions or reactions to what appeared to be their "child's calling in life." The adoptive parents of George Washington Carver refused to let him bring plants into the house. The parents of Thomas Edison bought him a chemistry set and hired a tutor to aid in his development; and the fathers of Florence Nightingale, Mozart, and Oprah Winfrey responded by taking a hands-on approach focusing specifically on their child's expressed interest. As part of Oprah's development, her grandmother not only taught her grand-daughter to read and write at the age of three, she also gave her positive re-enforcement by prophesying that one day her grand-daughter "will do wonderful things for others."

It is also important to note that many of the individuals featured in this book faced similar problems and circumstances that our modern-day teenagers are forced to deal with on a daily basis. Some were bored with school and called "lazy," others skipped classes or were considered unpopular, unattractive, and unwanted. There was the illegitimate son of a young peasant girl, she was forced to give him up at birth, and so like many young people today, this individual grew up never knowing his real mother. There was the rich girl who rejected her parents' plans for her to live a life of luxury; she chose instead a life of service to help the sick and afflicted. For those teens who were born in poverty, there was a sickly young child who was born a slave with no schooling; he was forced to use his God-given imagination to do the impossible. And finally, there were the brave, heroic teenagers that history either ignored or completely discounted; and despite it all, they made significant contributions that impacted the world.

Throughout the ages our young people have given us so much, from sacrificing their lives as soldiers to secure our freedom, to creating a multitude of products and services that made our world a better place in which to live. If we were to somehow eliminate or erase all of their contributions, our world and our lives as we know them, would be radically different.

Oprah Winfrey

The teenager who was molested
and rejected but touched the
lives of millions

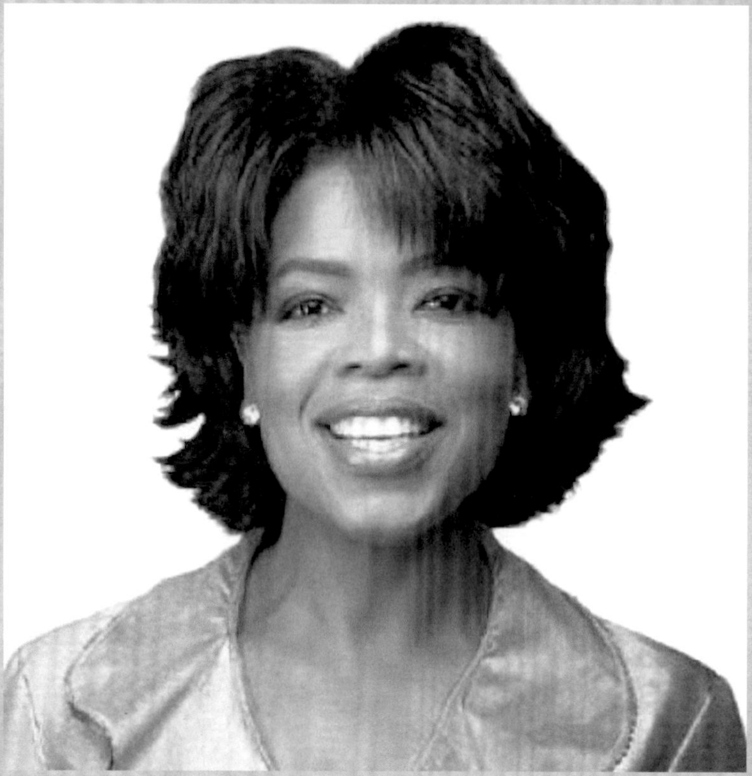

From Modern Times to Ancient Times

She was sexually molested as a child, pregnant at the age of fourteen, bounced from one home to the next (with one attempt to place her in a home for troubled teens), and still by the age of eighteen she became Miss Black Tennessee, started a career in radio broadcasting (WVOL), and at the age nineteen, a career in television with WTVF in Nashville, Tennessee. Today Oprah Gail Winfrey is not only the top television talk show host in America, but one of the most powerful and charitable women in the world.

She was born to Vernita Lee and Vernon Winfrey, two unwed teenagers, on January 29, 1954, in the small town of Kosciusko, Mississippi. With little resources to care for their new born, Oprah would spend the first five years of her life living with her grandmother on a small farm in Mississippi. Under the watchful care of her grandmother, the child felt safe, protected and "very special" even though they had very little. At the age of six, her dream life with her grandmother turned into a nightmare when she moved to Milwaukee to live with her biological mother (Vernita). By the age of thirteen, she had been rejected by her mother, molested by a friend and raped by a cousin. Feeling violated and abused, she trusted no one and became a very bitter, angry and rebellious child. On several occasions she attempted to run away from home. Her mother tried to place her in an institution for troubled teens but their facility was filled to capacity and they turned away the wayward child. By the age of fourteen she was pregnant, but lost her son in childbirth. This painful experience had a profound impact on her life and created a deep desire to change and change did come after she moved to Nashville, Tennessee, to live with her father.

Her gift of verbal communication was realized at a very early age when friends and family members heard her reciting stories and sermons at the age of three. Other speaking opportunities would come shortly after coming to live with her father, who, like Oprah's grandmother, protected her and took her to church on a regular basis. Through Sunday school and other children's programs, the church provided a multitude of opportunities for young Oprah to perfect her public speaking skills, and her father's strict reading requirements (with limited TV), meant she would have plenty to talk about. The weekly trips to the library paid off when she was offered a college scholarship at Tennessee State University, where she would major in speech communications and performing arts.

This unique problem child from the deep racist south who had very few childhood friends, went on to be one of the most powerful women in America, receiving a multitude of awards and recognition along the way. In 1986 she received The Woman of Achievement Award from the National Organization for Women. By 2002, she had been the recipient of the following awards:

The Bob Hope Humanitarian Award

The NAACP Spingnard Medal

Two People's Choice Awards

The National Academy of Television Arts and Sciences' 1998 Lifetime Achievement Award

From Modern Times to Ancient Times

The George Foster Peabody Award

The International Radio and Television Society Foundation's Gold Medal Award

The National Book Foundation's Fiftieth Anniversary Gold Medal

The NAACP's Image Award (four years running)

And the NAACP's 1989 Entertainer of the Year Award

 Oprah's humble beginnings as a child and her struggles as a teenager left an indelible impression on her life along with a deep compassion for others. In 1987, she established the Oprah Winfrey Foundation as a means to "support the inspiration, empowerment and education of women, children, and families around the world." And, having being abused as a child and fully aware of the thousands of children that are abused each year, she campaigned to establish a national database to track and identify child abusers. In December of 1993, President Bill Clinton signed "Oprah's Bill," officially known as the National Child Protection Act, an act establishing a national registry of convicted child abusers.

 Her Angel Network funded scholarships through the Boys and Girls Clubs of America; built homes for those in need through Habitat for Humanity; inspired thousands of individuals to create their "own miracle[s]" by making a difference in the lives of others; and, for those who were making a difference, Oprah sponsored the *Use Your Life Award*, which provided monetary awards to fund such causes.

 By September of 2002, Oprah's Angel Network had raised over $12 million, $5.1 million from viewer donations and $7 million from celebrities and corporate sponsors. With these funds the Angel Network:

- Provided scholarships for 150 students
- Funded over 200 homes through Habitat for Humanity
- Built thirty-four schools in ten countries with her Kids Can Free the Children program
- Presented over 50 <u>Use Your Life Awards,</u> totaling over $4 million.

Additionally, in December 2002, she established the Oprah Winfrey Leadership Academy for Girls in South Africa with a gift of $10 million from her own foundation. Other organizations that have been the recipients of her generosity include several historically black colleges and universities, the United Negro College Fund, the Harold Washington Library, Chicago Academy for the Arts, Chicago Public Schools, and her alma mater, Tennessee State University. Realizing the importance of reading and the impact that it had on her own life was perhaps the inspiration behind Oprah's Book Club, a program to encourage friends and fans to read for entertainment and inspiration.

On April 27, 2009, Time Magazine listed Oprah (the rebellious teenager that her mother rejected and friends molested) as one of the "100 Most Influential People of the Twentieth Century." Her powerful influence was manifested in 2008, when she gave her endorsement to a young, up-and-coming politician, and within months he became the first African American president of the United States.

From Modern Times to Ancient Times

    Every great person can point to one person who had a profound impact on their life. For Oprah it was Hattie Mae, Oprah's grandmother. Hattie Mae was the grandmother who taught her to read and write by age three; she was the one that took her to church every Sunday; and she was the spiritual angel that prophesied that one day her grand-daughter will "do wonderful things for others." Oprah says it is because of this godly woman of wisdom that she "reads the Bible every day" and gets down on her knees and "prays every night". Oprah proudly boasts, "I am what I am because of my grandmother."

    Pregnant, abused, molested and rejected, this powerful determined teenager who confessed that she reads the Bible every day and gets down on her knees to pray - turned her stumbling blocks into stepping stones and built a stairway to success.

Learning Through Life's Pains

I walked a mile with Pleasure,
And she chattered all the way.
But left me none the wiser,
For all she had to say.

Then I walked a mile with Sorrow,
And not a word said she.
But oh the things I learned from her,
When Sorrow walked with me.

                                            Author Unknown

Bill Gates

The teenager who caused problems in school while creating solutions in technology

Photo Courtesy of Doug Wilson

From Modern Times to Ancient Times

Although Bill Gates and Oprah Winfrey had very different backgrounds, they have two things in common: they both became billionaires despite the lack of support during portions of their childhood, and at a very young age they both loved to read. It was reported that at the age of eight, young Bill committed to reading every volume of the *World Book Encyclopedia* and succeeded up to the letter "P" before giving up.

At the age of 13, he was introduced to, and became fascinated with, the world of computers, it was a fascination that would not only make him one of the richest men on earth, but would radically change life on earth and the philanthropic spirit among the wealthiest persons on earth.

It was in 1968 when Gates was first introduced to computers. The introduction took place at Lakeside Prep in Seattle, Washington where he attended school. As his contagious excitement heightened for this new technology, other students became infected and formed an informal group of knowledge seekers. Among them were classmates Kent Evans and Paul Allen. It was Allen and Gates, who later co-founded the Microsoft Corporation, employing over 30,000 employees around the world.

Bill's obsession with computer technology meant that his side interests of roller-skating, tennis, skiing and playing card games with his parents, would have to take a backseat. Fellow students recall how Bill and other students would remain in the computer room day and night writing programs, reading computer literature and doing anything they could to increase their knowledge of this newfound technology. It wasn't long before Gates and his classmates started running into problems with the faculty. Their homework was being turned in late (if at all), they were skipping classes to spend time in the computer room and worst of all, they had used up all the computer time that was allotted to the school by the Computer Center Corporation (CCC), a new computer company in Seattle.

CCC had formed a relationship with Lakeside, a relationship that provided free computer time for their students. Gates and his teenage buddies ignored the terms and conditions of this relationship and started abusing the privileges set forth in the agreement. They broke the computer's security system, caused the system to crash several times and altered the files that recorded and documented computer usage. When they were caught, CCC banned them from using the computers for several weeks.

Later that year, Gates and Allen along with two other classmates formed the Lakeside Programmers Group (LPG). When CCC started experiencing problems with their system, they hired Gates and his newly formed LPG group to find computer bugs and other weaknesses in their system. In exchange for the group's services, the company gave them unlimited computer time. Although the group was hired to find computer bugs, the inquisitive teenagers seized the opportunity to read any and all computer related literature that the day shift had left behind.

After CCC closed their doors in 1970 due to financial problems, Information Sciences Inc. (ISI) hired the teenagers (LPG) to program a payroll system for their company. Again the group was given free computer time and for the first time, a source of income. ISI had agreed to pay royalties from the profits generated from the sale of their programs. As a result of this business arrangement, the young group of high school computer geniuses became legitimate business professionals.

During Gates' junior year at Lakeside, the administration gave him an assignment to computerize the school's scheduling system. After he and Paul Allen completed the project (during the summer months), Gates and Allen sought other opportunities to use their skills as a source of income and soon started their own company, Traf-O-Data. One of their first contracts involved designing a special program to help measure the flow of highway traffic. From this project they grossed approximately $20,000. Opportunity knocked again during their senior year, when Traf-O-Data was contacted by TRF, a defense contractor that was plagued with a bug-infested computer system similar to the problem that Computer Center Corporation had encountered. TRW hired the two teenagers, which added to their resumes and broadened their experience. In the fall of 1973, Traf-O-Data was forced to close its doors when Gates left for Boston to attend Harvard University.

Bill was born into a prominent family in Seattle, Washington on October 28, 1955. His great-grandfather had been a state legislator and mayor, his grandfather was the vice president of a national bank, and his father was a member of a prestigious law firm. As a child, Bill surpassed all of his classmates in nearly all subjects, particularly in the areas of math and science. After dropping out of Harvard University in 1975 at the age of 20, Bill Gates and Paul Allen formed the most powerful software company in the world (Microsoft) and revolutionized the computer industry.

This former teenage genius, who was now committed to developing software products that would transform the business world, was equally committed to helping those who were less fortunate throughout the world. Many believe his compassion for others came from his mother who devoted much of her lifetime to charitable work and to serving others. According to the a story printed in the *New York Times* on April 16, 2000, Bill and his wife Melinda have given billions "to improve the health and the quality of life for students, world health organizations and educators." The following are a few of the grant commitments made by the Bill and Melinda Gates Foundation from 1994 to March of 2011.

Program Areas	
Global Development	$3,277,000,000
Global Health	$14,492,000,000
United States	$ 6,005,000,000
Non Program Grants	
Charitable Sector Support	$56,000,000
Employee Matching Gifts & Sponsorship	$20,000,000
Family Interest	$962,000,000
Total Grants	$24,812,000,000

The young man, who wrote his first computer program at the age thirteen in a private school in Seattle, used his gifts, his talents, and his heart of compassion to touch the lives of billions around the world.

Rosa Parks & Young Claudette Colvin

The defiant teenager who stood up for equality when she sat down

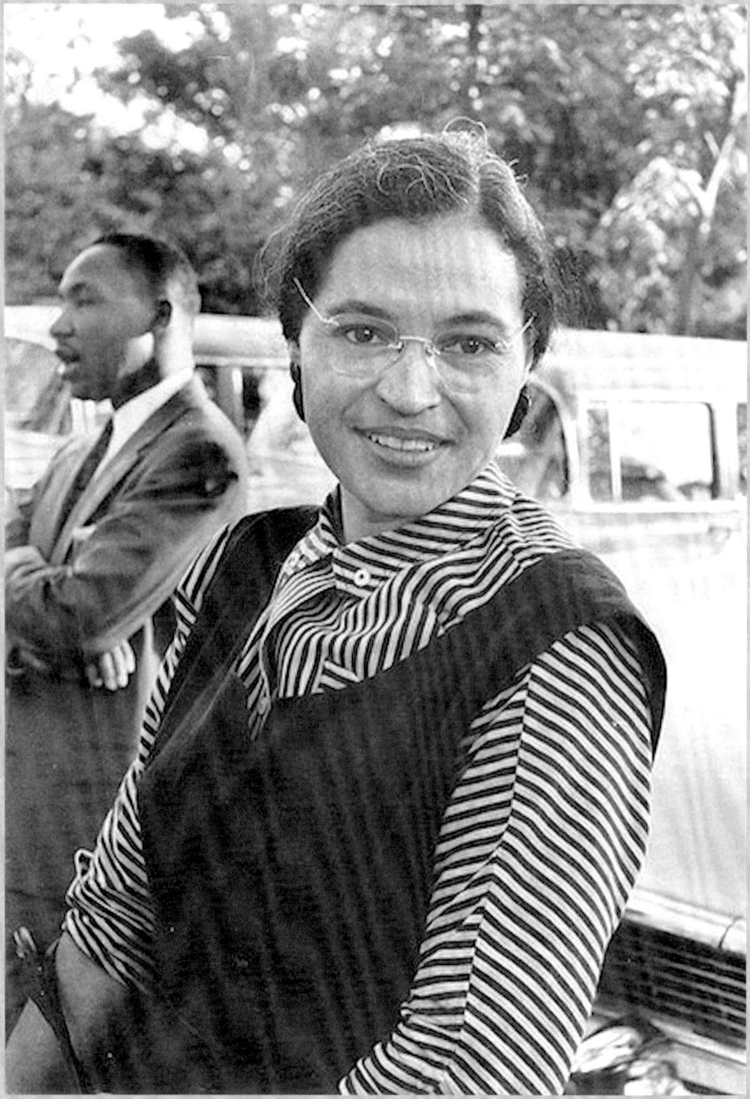

She was a tired fifteen-years-old student attending Booker T. Washington High School in Montgomery, Alabama on March 2, 1955, when she refused to give up her seat (on the bus) for a white passenger. Claudette Colvin was her name and her defiance to the Democrat's segregated policies in the South took place approximately nine months prior to Rosa Parks' refusal to do the same (December 1, 1955).

Claudette was sitting near the emergency exit when four whites boarded the bus. The driver ordered the teenager, along with three other black passengers, to give up their seats. When Claudette refused, she was handcuffed and forcibly removed from the bus by two white police officers and charged with assault and violating the city's ordinances on segregation. During the hearing, in response to the charges by the police that young Claudette had resisted arrest by refusing to cooperate and "spewed out curse words," Claudette's schoolmate; Annie Larkins Price testified that her friend "didn't say anything, she just stared out the window, determined not to give up her seat."

The teenager and Rosa Parks weren't strangers; they were both members of and worked with their local chapter of the NAACP (National Association for the Advancement of Colored People). Claudette was active in the NAACP's Youth Council. People who knew them well reported that Claudette's mother and Ms. Parks were childhood friends, and as children, they had often played together.

When Claudette was arrested, the Montgomery chapter of the NAACP went into action. The civil rights organization had been waiting for a test case to challenge the city's racist policies and vowed to take action on behalf of the teenager. Claudette's father and many other members of the community (including Rosa Parks) started raising funds for her defense.

Their fund-raising effort was cancelled abruptly when it was alleged that young Claudette was pregnant by a much-older married man. The NAACP and local leaders felt the southern press would have a field day with this immoral transgression and dropped their support. Church leaders in this deeply religious black community withdrew their support as well. As a result, Claudette was convicted in juvenile court of violating the laws of segregation and assault.

Looking back over time, many historians are now convinced that it was young Claudette's refusal to give up her seat that motivated Rosa Parks to do the same nine months later. When Ms. Parks refused to give up her seat, local leaders rallied around Parks and launched the Montgomery Bus Boycott. The boycott was led by a fairly unknown preacher at the time, the Reverend Dr. Martin Luther King Jr.

Like Claudette Colvin, Rosa Parks also lost her case. While the Parks' decision was under appeal in the state courts of Alabama, Civil Rights attorneys Fred Gray, E.D. Nixon and Clifford Durr decided to search for a new case to file in federal court. Durr was a white civil rights activist and a friend of Rosa Parks. After consulting with Thurgood Marshall (who later became the first African American to serve on the U.S. Supreme Court), the three attorneys contacted four women, Aurelia Browder, Susie McDonald, Mary Louise Smith, and who else but young Claudette Colvin, to be the plaintiffs in what would become one of the most important civil rights cases in American history, *Browder v. Gayle* (Gayle was the mayor of Montgomery). All four women were victims of Montgomery's racist bus policies.

On February 1, 1956, eleven months after Claudette's refusal to give up her seat, the case of *Browder v Gayle* was filed in U.S. District Court by attorney Fred Gray. It was sixteen-year-old Claudette Colvin and the three other plaintiffs who were the key witnesses in this landmark case, not Rosa Parks. On June 19, 1956, the United States District Court of Alabama ruled in favor of the plaintiffs (see Appendix I for the written decision).

While history has honored Rosa Parks, it has consistently ignored the teenage girl who inspired Rosa Parks and gave her the courage to do what young Claudette had done nine months prior. In addition to never acknowledging the contributions of this teenager, history has never given the young girl credit for being courageous enough to be one of the key plaintiffs in the case that broke the back of segregation in Montgomery and eventually destroyed the Democrats' segregation policies of the South. In 1956, being a key plaintiff in a race-related case in the south could have resulted in her death. Nevertheless, she was determined to challenge and change the system. Claudette Colvin's actions, not only changed the South, it push the civil rights movement to the forefront and changed America forever.

Teens and Young People Who Impacted the World

  According to actress Awele Makeba, who produced the stage play: "*Rage Is Not a 1 Day Thing,*" (a play about Claudette's life), "Claudette gave birth to her son, Raymond, shortly after giving her testimony (in 1956). In 1958, she moved to New York and worked for over thirty years in a Catholic nursing home. Ms. Colvin retired in 2004 after thirty-five years of working as a nurse's assistant." Claudette Colvin was born on September 5, 1939, retiring at the age of sixty-five.

The Teens & Dr. King

**The determined teenagers who
fought against racism
in the South and for equality
in Congress**

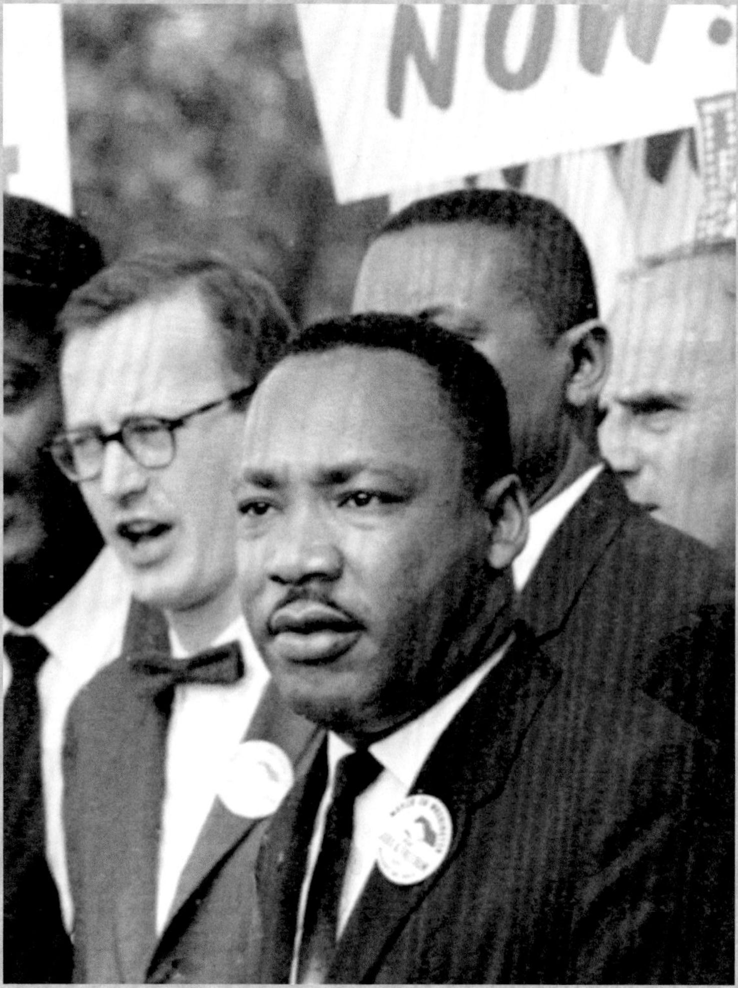
NOW

From Modern Times to Ancient Times

When he was child, no one had to tell him what segregation was. He grew up in a region that had been controlled by one political party from the time of slavery through the Jim Crow lynching era of the 1970s. The chronicles of history reveal that every southern state, county, city, town and community was controlled by thousands of Democratic governors, mayors, congressmen, legislators, law enforcement officers and judges. From 1877 to 1977, over 300 Democrat governors ruled the southern states of Alabama, Arkansas, Florida, Kentucky, Mississippi, Louisiana, Tennessee, Texas, Virginia, North Carolina, South Carolina, Oklahoma and Georgia (see Appendix II for list). The southern region of the United States was an area where blacks and whites lived in different neighborhoods, drank from separate water fountains, used different restrooms and attended different schools. It was a region where there were two distinct societies, one black and one white.

Little Michael knew that he had a calling on his life, and that one day things would be different. Michael was his birth name, but his father later changed his name, naming him after the great reformer, Martin Luther (and himself Sr.). Today we know him as the Reverend. Dr. Martin Luther King Jr., even though some claim they never *legally* changed his name. Born January 15, 1929, in Atlanta, Georgia, just ten years before Claudette Colvin, young Michael attended David T. Howard Elementary School and graduated from Booker T. Washington High School at the age of fifteen. Upon graduation, he applied and was accepted at Morehouse College in Atlanta, Georgia. With a degree in sociology at the age of nineteen, he went on to study religion at Crozer Theological Seminary in Upland, Pennsylvania as part of the final preparation for the work that he would be known for.

After successfully leading the Montgomery Bus Boycotts in Alabama (which led to the *Bower* decision, the case that involved Claudette Colvin), Dr. King's nonviolent efforts during the next four years (1956-1960) failed to produce any *major* pieces of civil rights legislation. Southern whites were just as defiant and racism was still alive and well. While many of the older generation (both black and white), thought he (Dr. King) was a "troublemaker" and his mission was hopeless, the younger generation felt that change must come and must come "by any means possible."

Historians now acknowledge that it wasn't the older generation that pushed the civil rights movement to the forefront. Most of them were so fearful of retaliation that they refused to open their homes to house the civil rights workers from the north. It was high school students, college students and individuals like John Lewis, who gave the movement new life with the formation of the Student Nonviolent Coordinating Committee (SNCC) and other similar groups. History records that it was the teenagers from local high schools and colleges who brought about the increased numbers that would fill the streets during public protests and unforgettable civil rights marches. They were the ones (not the older generation) who initiated the lunch counter protests, and risked their lives to integrate schools, businesses and register new black voters. Many believe that without these brave young souls, Dr. King's nonviolent movement would have hit a permanent roadblock and died.

Although Dr. King had the support of the older generation during the Montgomery Bus Boycotts in 1955, it was young Claudette Colvin's federal case that sealed the deal on the boycotts and it was four nineteen year old freshmen known as the "Greensboro Four" from the North Carolina Agricultural and Technical College who sparked the dying civil rights movement with what would be known as "*sit-ins*." On February 1, 1960, exactly four years after the *Bowder case* was filed, Joseph McNeil, Franklin McCain, David Richmond, and Ezell Blair Jr. walked into the F. W. Woolworth store (similar to today's K-Mart stores) and launched the first *sit-in*.

After shopping for school supplies, the four went to the lunch counter (for white customers only) and asked to be served. When the store employees refused to serve them, they left, only to return the next day with a larger group of students. The older generation was furious and advised their teenagers not to take part in "such nonsense." But the teenagers rejected their counsel and continued. When the Congress of Racial Equality (CORE) heard about the efforts of these brave students (in the midst of a violent, racist South), they sent young representatives from New York to support them. In less than two weeks, students in eleven cities held *sit-ins* at other southern stores, including S.H. Kress (Woolworth's competitor). During the next six months over 70,000 persons participated in the *sit-ins* and more than 3,000 were arrested.

Teens and Young People Who Impacted the World

By 1962, Dr. King's Southern Christian Leadership Conference (SCLC) and the NAACP weren't the only groups that were making headlines. They now had to share the spotlight with the young members of CORE, SNCC, and the Freedom Riders. When Dr. King tried to form an alliance with SNCC by proposing that they become a division of his organization (Southern Christian Leadership Conference), the young students rejected the idea.

While many young people respected Dr. King, others openly criticized him. In the book, *Martin Luther King: I Have A Dream: Writing & Speeches,* James M. Washington made the following observation: "It hurt him [Dr. King] greatly to receive criticism from some of his Student Nonviolent Coordinating Committee colleagues after their 1962 voter registration campaign" (p. 83). Others wrote about the divide between Dr. King and the student organization as well, including Dr. King's friend, Harris Wofford, the Special Assistant to President John F. Kennedy for Civil Rights. In his book: *Of Kennedy's and Kings: Making Sense of The Sixties,* Wofford states the following about Dr. King and SNCC:

> "When the Student Nonviolent Coordinating Committee, including Julian Bond and Marion Barry, proposed a *sit-in* against segregation in restaurants and lunch counters in downtown Atlanta stores, King urged a delay until after the [Presidential] election. When the young militants decided to

go ahead anyway King tried to arrange to be out of town on the day that the *sit-ins* were scheduled" (p.12).

"…He [King] had launched a Crusade for Citizenship to register five million Southern Negroes; and it had floundered, but the plan was still close to King's heart. He had had enough doubts about the tactics of the Freedom Riders so that he never rode himself. Instead, King told the Southern Christian Leadership Conference to start planning for a registration drive. Later in the summer of 1961, when the SNCC students were torn by the question of whether to turn away from direct action to the voting drive, many of them felt King was being "co-opted by the Kennedys." (p. 159)

[Note: The Freedom Riders were groups bussed from the North to assist SNCC with their desegregation efforts in the south, although adults participated, most were young people.]

While SNCC encouraged and used techniques of nonviolence to accomplish their goals, from 1961 to 1963 the country was in a state of chaos and social unrest. Seeing young people beaten and arrested (on national TV) during a non-violent Children's March in Birmingham in 1963, resulted in a wave of protests and riots throughout the country. When southern law enforcement officials released their vicious police dogs and used powerful water hoses to attack the young protesters, it lit a match that ignited an unquenchable fire and young people from inner cities

Teens and Young People Who Impacted the World

across America took to the streets. King's worst fears were now being realized. Some called the protestors "hoodlums," other called them "thugs" (and some were), but most were young people who were tired of the horrific racist conditions in the South, tired of double-digit black unemployment, and tired of seeing their parents and grandparents submitting to white authority with their heads bowed low and with fearful responses of "yes sir boss."

Parents warned their children not to get involved, fearing violent repercussions. Their worst fears were realized when the bodies of four little girls attending Sunday school were found in the basement of the 16th Street Baptist Church in Birmingham, Alabama after a Sunday morning bombing; and when the three young bodies of James Chaney, Michael Schwerner, and Andrew Goodman were found at a dump site in Mississippi. Of the three young men, two were out-of-state college students from New York who came down to Mississippi to assist with voter registration; the other was a local resident. These violent acts may have deterred older blacks, who were fearful, but it only made the younger generation who were fearless, more determined and they took to the streets.

The massive protests caught the attention of President John F. Kennedy and the United States Congress. On June 19, 1963, President Kennedy acknowledged the social chaos in his letter to Congress. The following are portions of that letter:

> "Last week I addressed to the American people an appeal to conscience — a request for their

cooperation in meeting the growing moral crisis in American race relations. I warned of "a rising tide of discontent that threatens the public safety" in many parts of the country. I emphasized that "the events in Birmingham and elsewhere have so increased the cries for equality that no city or state or legislative body can prudently choose to ignore them." "It is a time to act," I said, "in the Congress, in State and local legislative bodies and, above all, in all of our daily lives."

In the days that have followed, the predictions of increased violence have been tragically borne out. "The fires of frustration and discord have burned hotter than ever...."

"...The result of continued Federal legislative inaction will be continued, if not increased, racial strife — causing the leadership on both sides to pass from the hands of reasonable responsible men to the purveyors of hate and violence, endangering domestic tranquility, retarding our nation's economic and social progress and weakening the respect with which the rest of the world regards us. No American, I feel sure, would prefer this course of tension, disorder and division — and the great majority of our citizens simply cannot accept it...."

"For these reasons, I am proposing that the Congress stay in session this year until it has enacted — preferably as a single omnibus bill — the most responsible, reasonable, and urgently needed solutions to this problem, solutions which should be acceptable to all fair-minded men. This bill would be known as the Civil Rights Act of 1963 ...."

Unlike Dr. King's nonviolent efforts which received very little press coverage, the young people's riots and public protests received <u>worldwide media coverage</u> as indicated in Kennedy's letter to Congress when he stated that the protests were "weakening the respect with which the rest of <u>the world regards us</u>."

A number of southern Democrats thought their Democratic president (President Kennedy) was giving in to a bunch of young "criminals." They strongly expressed how they felt during the debates over the newly proposed Civil Rights Act of 1963 (which, after the assassination of Kennedy, became the Civil Rights Act of 1964). The debates lasted over eighty days, it resulted in over 7,000 pages of Congressional transcripts (consisting of over 10 million words), and created the longest filibuster in U.S. Senate history. The filibuster was led by Democratic Senator, Al Gore Sr. of Tennessee. From the debates it was evident that southern Democrats were more concerned with the riots initiated by the youth in America, than they were with their party's historical treatment of African Americans (they had supported slavery and Jim Crow). The following are some of the arguments and threats posed by key southern Democrats during those debates.

Thomas Abernethy, a Democrat from Mississippi, argued,

"If enacted [Civil Rights Act of 1964], it is certain to precipitate a tremendous upheaval in our society, but not the kind of upheaval that proponents apparently expect. I predict it will precipitate an <u>upheaval that will make the sit-ins, kneel-ins, lie-ins, mass picketing, chanting, the march on Washington</u>, and all other elements of the so-called Negro revolutions, all of these – I predict – will look like kindergarten play in comparison with the counter-revolution that is bound to arise and continue to grow and grow, and grow."

Richard Russell, a Democrat from Georgia, told Congress,

"This bill contains a number of provisions that had never been requested by President John F. Kennedy, and some provisions that he had publicly adjudged as being improper and unconstitutional. …It was only after <u>a long series of demonstrations and unfortunate acts of violence</u> that he [President Kennedy] finally succumbed to this tremendous pressure <u>brought to bear by all the various groups</u> of extreme left wing and minority groups [SCLC CORE, SNCC, NAACP] and asked for a bill bearing the label of civil rights. …It is one of the most far-reaching and drastic pieces of legislation ever to be presented to the American Congress. …If this bill should be passed, it would drastically change our entire system. It would turn our social order upside down. It would have a tremendous impact on what we have called, in happier times, the American way of life."

Howard Smith, a Democrat from Virginia, added the following arguments:

"I deeply regret that out of the 15 minutes allotted to me, I cannot assign time for protest to the many patriotic Members of this House who would like to express their distaste, dismay and disgust at this invasion of the rights of American citizens. In a few minutes, you will vote this monstrous instrument of oppression upon all of the American People.... Be forewarned that <u>the paid agents and leaders of the NAACP</u> can never permit this law to be gradually and peacefully accepted because that means an end to their well-paid activities."

Olin Johnston, the Democrat from South Carolina argued,

"Mr. President, this is indeed the blackest day in the U.S. Senate since 1875, when Congress passed a civil rights bill similar to this one. It was 89 years ago that the [Republican] Congress passed the nefarious Reconstruction era civil rights laws, identical with what we are now discussing, which were later declared unconstitutional by the U.S. Supreme Court. The Senate, if it passes this measure before us, will be compounding that unconstitutional error made back in 1875 [when Republicans passed the 1875 Civil Rights Act]. I predict that this bill will never be enforced <u>without turning our Nation into a police state and without the cost of bloodshed and violence.</u>"

The feelings expressed during the debates were similar to those expressed by Senator Ben Tillman of South Carolina who told his colleagues, "We reorganized the Democrat Party with one plank and one plank only, namely, <u>that this is a white man's country and white men must govern it.</u>" While these types of statements and arguments frightened older blacks, they only made younger blacks furious. So furious, that Fannie Lou Hamer and several other young people from SNCC formed the Mississippi Freedom Democratic Party (MFDP) to infiltrate the Democratic Party and change it from within. Their goal was to win seats at the 1964 Democratic National Convention and replace the Mississippi racist delegates with members from their group, but President Lyndon B. Johnson stood in their way. Historians say that Johnson used FBI Director, J. Edgar Hoover, prominent Democrats and even Dr. King to put pressure on the MFDP, but Fannie Lou and her MFDP organization refused to give in and continued their fight until they were heard. Fannie Lou Hamer was a devout Christian and a victim of the south's racist practice of sterilizing young black girls without their knowledge or permission. The south initiated these practices to <u>reduce the black voting population</u>. During the MFDP protests, neither Dr. King nor Fannie Lou, were aware of the comments that Johnson had made to his friend and colleague, Senator Richard Russell of Georgia. Johnson told Russell:

From Modern Times to Ancient Times

"These Negroes, they're getting pretty uppity these days and that's a problem for us since they got something now that they never had before, the political pull to back up their uppityness. Now we've got to do something about this, we've got to <u>give them a little something, just enough to quiet them down, not enough to make a difference</u>. For if we don't move at all, then their allies [Republicans] will line up against us and there'll be no way of stopping them, we'll lose the filibuster and there'll be no way of putting a brake on all sorts of wild legislation. It'll be Reconstruction all over again."
(p. 148 <u>Lyndon Johnson and the American Dream</u>)

Johnson was right; there was "no way of stopping them." Through the formation of the MDFP, the aggressive black youth were successful in infiltrating the Democratic Party of the south. Their efforts paid off in 1973 when Barbara Jordan (from Texas) became the Democrat's first black elected member of Congress from the south. The victory came almost ten years after the passage of the Civil Rights Act of 1964. Forty-seven years later (2011), a group of African Americans from the civil rights era of the sixties, filed suit against the Democratic Party, demanding that they issue a public apology to African Americans for the party's past racist practices and their support of slavery. The leadership of the Democratic Party, while not denying their racist history and the numerous allegations cited in the Plaintiffs' brief, refused to issue an apology and hired the prestigious law firm of Perkins and Coie (in Seattle, Washington) to represent them.

One of the members of SNCC summed up the youth's contribution to the civil rights movement this way, he said: "Over and over throughout the 1960's, black and other anti-racist teenagers and younger youth were often the unsung heroes of the movements for equality and social justice. Despite the decisive role youth played in making it possible for the past movements to win its victories, most historians have ignored their contributions." The young people's relentless efforts in pursuit of equality (for all mankind) resulted in the passage of the Civil Rights Act of 1964, an act that provided equality and protection for African Americans, Latinos, Native Americans, Asians, women, the handicapped and persons over forty, all of which transformed the American culture. In 1964, Dr. King was recognized and awarded the Nobel Peace Prize for his tremendous work, but the efforts and the supportive role that the young people played in King's success went un-noticed. One day the chronicles of history will give credence to the fact, that without the support of the fearless teens, King's dream would have turned into a nightmare.

Teenagers: America's Young Warriors

The courageous teens who made "one nation under God" a reality

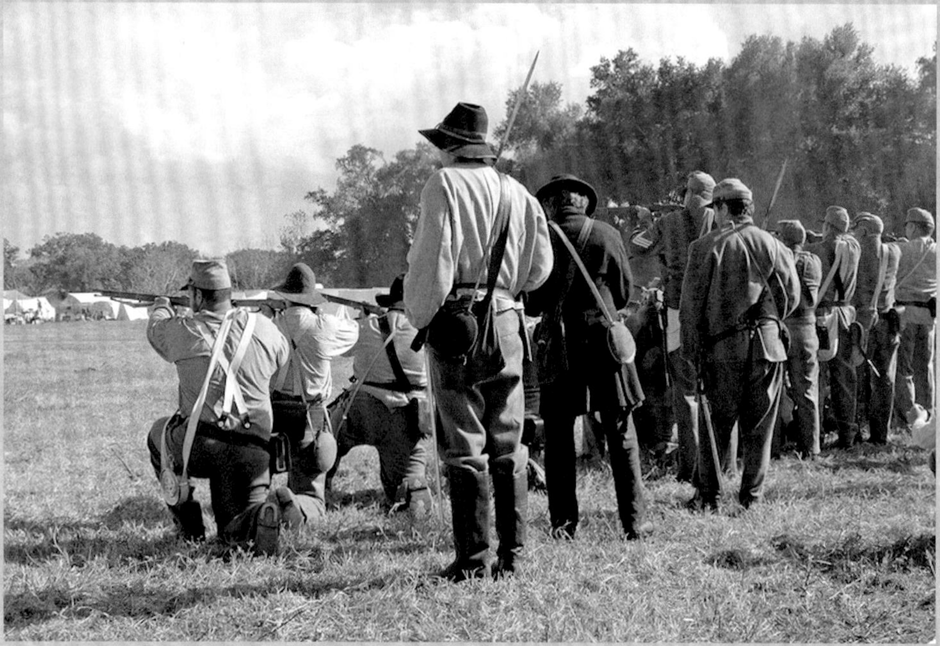

From Modern Times to Ancient Times

The civil rights movement of the 60's was not the first time that the actions of America's youth made a difference. Over **234,000** teenagers fought in the Civil War to end slavery. The following is a break-down by age:

Age 13 = 127
Age 14 = 330
Age 15 = 773
Age 16 = 2,758
Age 17 = 6,425
Age 18 = 133,475
Age 19 = 90,215

History tells us that Lincoln was the only president in our nation's history that was faced with the possibility of a future where there would be at least two separate nations rather than the one that our founding fathers had established. Using teenage soldiers to win the war and unite the country was a tremendous accomplishment and that alone should make Lincoln the greatest president of all times. Had he allowed the South to exist as a separate nation, and had we remained as two smaller countries instead of the one we know today, becoming a superpower would have only been a dream and never a reality. As two separate (smaller and weaker) nations, our capacity to defend democracies around the world would have been greatly diminished, and this diminished capacity would have changed the course of history.

Teens and Young People Who Impacted the World

During the past two decades, while many college administrators argued whether or not military recruiters should be allowed on America's college campuses, they overlooked the fact that without our young soldiers, our nation never would have gained its independence, ended slavery, or defeated foreign dictators. The role that our young men and women played in our nation's conflicts was significant and cannot be ignored.

It could be said that the freedom we currently enjoy, was paid for with the blood of those teenagers and college-age-students who were willing to give their lives *"so* [as in the words of Abraham Lincoln] *that - that nation might live...."* From the time that the military draft was established by President Lincoln in 1863 to this present date, we have never seen military recruiters seeking recruits from our nation's retirement homes and rest homes; high school and college-age students has always been their focus.

As we look to the future, we know that America's future and freedom will be contingent and dependent on its military might, and as in time past, many of the young warriors will be teenagers. Today, over fourteen million young men and women are registered for the draft. Not only will America rely on them, our ally nations around the world will also look to them to secure their safety and freedoms as well.

Albert Einstein

The strange un-attractive lazy teen who won respect around the world

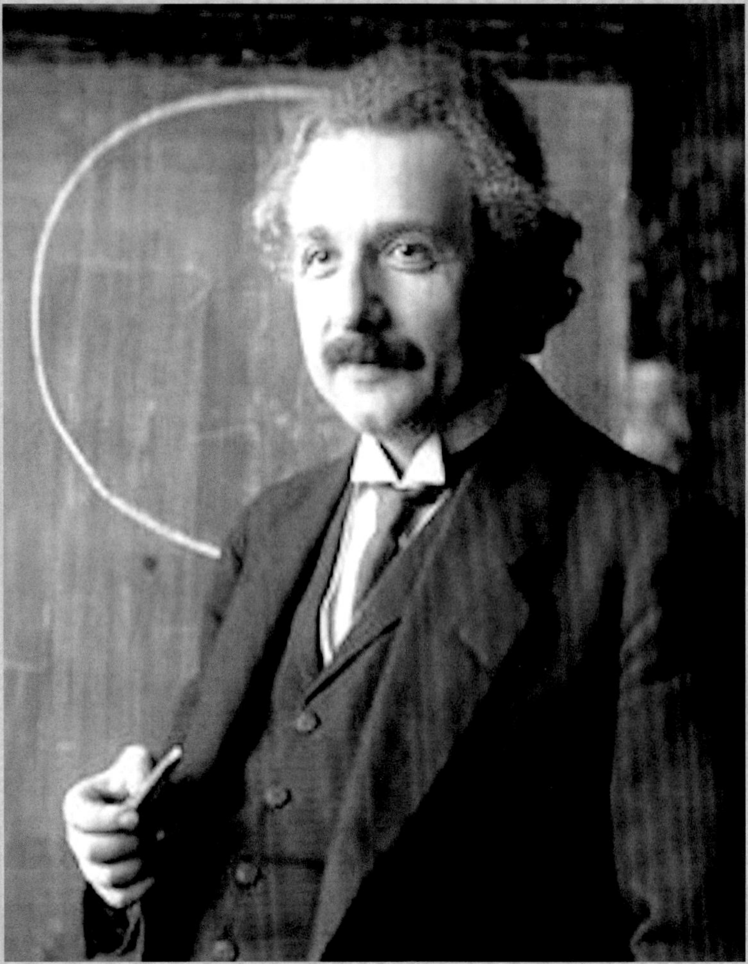

From Modern Times to Ancient Times

The problem child with a strangely shaped head, who like many other students today found school to be boring, knew what he wanted to do by the age of twelve. He was fascinated with the *behavior of the universe*. Albert recalled that when he was four or five years old, he would watch the needle on a magnetic compass, guided by an invisible force. As he watched, he knew there had to be something behind this unique phenomenon and he wanted to know what it was.

No matter how hard he tried, young Albert just didn't fit in. While other children played, Albert would just stare off into space or simply meditate while playing the violin, which he had mastered as a child. At the age of fifteen he took the advice of an *unfriendly tutor* and left school. Shortly after, at the age of seventeen, he managed to qualify for enrollment in the renowned Polytechnic in Zurich, Switzerland. Even there, his instructors referred to him as a *"lazy dog."* and said, *"He will never amount to anything."* This so-called *"lazy,"* strange child that few understood, one who was known for his slow speech (taking a pause to consider what he would say before responding), would eventually receive his doctorate degree in 1905, and go on to be one of the greatest scientists of all time.

Born at Ulm, in Württemberg, Germany, on March 14, 1879, Albert Einstein became Professor Extraordinary at Zurich by 1909, and the Professor of Theoretical Physics at Prague by 1911. In 1914, he was appointed Director of the Kaiser Wilhelm Physical Institute and Professor for the University of Berlin. In 1914, he became a German citizen and remained in Berlin until 1933, when he renounced his citizenship for political reasons and emigrated to America to take the position of Professor of Theoretical Physics at Princeton University.

The problem child with the strangely shaped head, not only had a fascination for the mysteries associated with the world of physics, he had the determination to solve them. His unique ability to visualize the main stages on the way to his goal was unprecedented.

His famous *theory of relativity* stemmed from an attempt to reconcile the laws of mechanics with the laws of the electromagnetic field. In 1916, he published his paper on the general theory of relativity. He dealt with classical problems of statistical mechanics and reviewed the previous research associated with the *quantum theory*. He investigated the wave length properties of light with a low radiation density and his observations laid the foundation of the *photon theory of light*.

On August 2, 1939, just before the beginning of World War II, Einstein sent a letter to President Franklin D. Roosevelt and told him of Nazi Germany's intentions to purify Uranium-235, which could be used to build an atomic bomb. It is believed that Einstein's revelations regarding Germany's intentions are what inspired the United States Government to start the Manhattan Project, a project that was committed to researching and producing America's own atomic bomb.

After World War II, Einstein was now a leading figure in the World Government Movement. So highly respected was he that he was offered the Presidency of the State of

From Modern Times to Ancient Times

Israel. He declined and collaborated with Dr. Chaim Weizmann in establishing the Hebrew University of Jerusalem.

Albert Einstein married Mileva Maric in 1903; they had a daughter and two sons. The two were divorced in 1919 and in the same year he married his cousin, Elsa Löwenthal, who died in 1936. The man who first became interested in science and physics at the age of four, died on April 18, 1955, in Princeton, New Jersey, at the age of seventy-six.

Despite how he looked or what people thought of him as a child, young Einstein stayed focused and determined, and eventually turned the subjective harsh criticism about his looks and intelligence, into expressions of praise.

Watch Your Mouth

Be careful of the words you say,
Keep them soft and sweet.
You never know from day to day.
Which ones you'll have to eat.

                                                Author Unknown

Jan Matzeliger

The lonely teenager without family and friends who found solutions for our feet

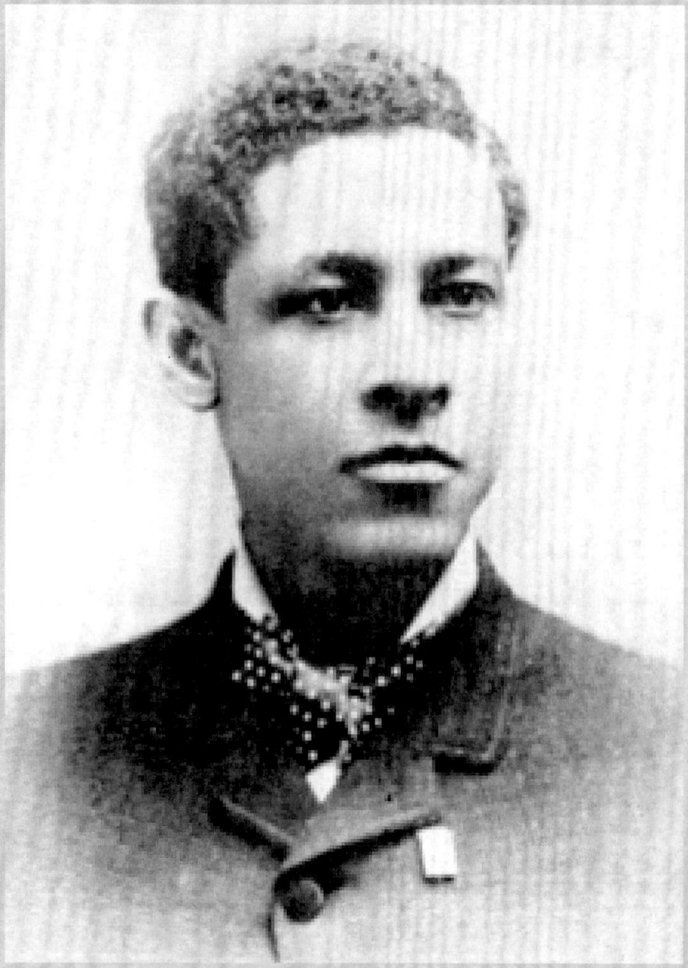

From Modern Times to Ancient Times

After serving nine years as an apprentice in a machine shop in Dutch Guiana (from ages ten through nineteen), Jan Matzeliger, the quiet intelligent son of a black slave woman and a white engineer, decided to take a voyage that would not only change his life but the lives of millions around the world.

In 1871, at the age nineteen, Jan took a merchant ship and sailed from Guiana to Lynn, Massachusetts where he landed a job as a shoe-stitching-machine operator. Although the Dutch-speaking black teenager visited several local churches, he found no solace among them, so he was forced to spend his time alone. He devoted his time of solitude to reading and studying the process of making shoes.

In those days, the shoe-making process included sewing the top of the shoe together before shaping the piece over a wooden model of a human foot, called "a last." Next, the craftsman would sew the top to the inner sole. It took great skill and strength to bend, shape, and hold the top portion of the shoe, while stitching it to the bottom. Sewing each shoe by hand took a considerable amount of time and skill.

For years, persons within the industry tried in vain to invent a machine that could improve the process. After many years of failures, it was Jan who finally found a mechanized solution. With very little money to work with, he found the parts and materials to build a prototype. Many times he worked ten- hour days and went without food so he could purchase more materials. After five years of intense study and research, he finally finished his project and filed a fifteen-page patent for what would be called, the Shoe Lasting Machine: a machine that revolutionized shoe manufacturing around the world.

The new machine could adjust the shoe, arrange the leather over the sole, and drive in nails to produce a finished product. The new machine cut shoe prices in half, cut the time of production by as much as 75 percent and made Lynn, Massachusetts the shoe capital of the world. Jan Matzeliger, who was born in 1852, sold the patent to Sydney W. Winslow, the president and founder of the United Shoe Machinery Company.

Jan died of tuberculosis at the age of thirty-seven. Prior to his death he had finally established some meaningful relationships with the members of the North Congregational Church where he taught Sunday school. He left his entire fortune to the church. It had been the first church to look beyond the color of his skin and see a person worthy of love. Every shoe manufacturer in the world owes their success in part to the intelligent ten year old boy who started as an apprentice in a machine shop in 1862.

Thomas Edison

The abused teenager with a physical handicap and a brilliant mind

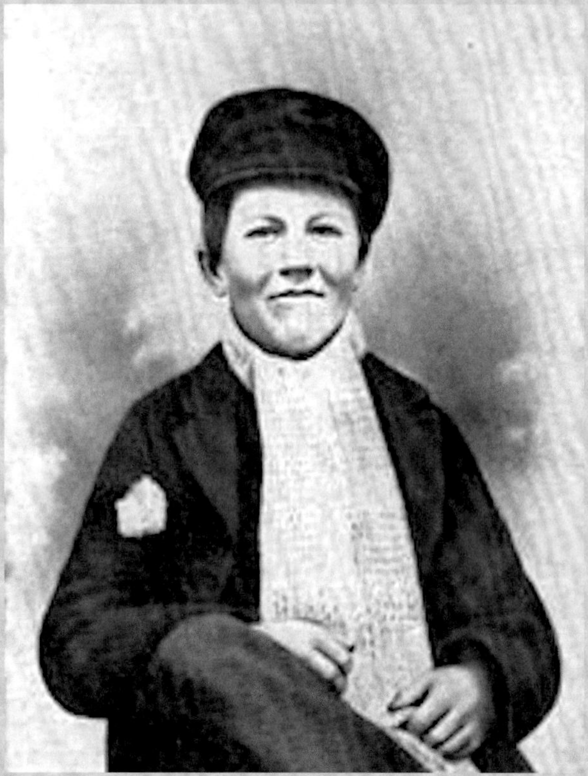

Being the youngest of seven children, young Thomas was home-schooled by his mother and encouraged to read the Bible and the great classics. In addition to his interest in world history, English literature, and Shakespeare, he had an equal interest in mechanical objects and the chemical make-up of chemical-based products.

When he became totally engrossed in science at the age of twelve, his parents scraped together enough money to buy him a chemistry set and hire a tutor. To purchase chemical supplies for his scientific experiments (which took place in his parents' basement), young Thomas developed several small business ventures including selling fruits and vegetables and distributing the Weekly Herald newspaper to passengers on trains.

At the age of fourteen, young Edison lost 80 percent of his hearing in one ear and became completely deaf in the other after a bout with scarlet fever, a hearing loss, which others say, was further aggravated by a blow to the head by an angry train conductor. His physical handicap didn't dampen his drive or his enthusiasm to succeed. In fact, it made him more determined.

At the age of sixteen, while working as a telegraph operator, he came up with his first invention: the automatic repeater, a device that transmitted telegraph signals between unmanned stations. The new invention allowed individuals to translate codes at their own rate of speed and at their own convenience. And this was the beginning of one of the greatest inventors in the world.

Teens and Young People Who Impacted the World

Thomas went on to invent many other products, including the predecessor to our present-day CD player. It was called "the phonograph" and later referred to as the "record player". This invention came about while young Edison was working to improve the efficiency of the telegraph transmitter. During the process he discovered that the tape from the machine generated a sound resembling spoken words when played at a high speed. He wondered if he could record a telephone message by using this same process. Taking the diaphragm of a telephone receiver and attaching a needle to it, he discovered that the needle could prick a paper tape to record a message. His first recording was a hip-hop style (talking version) of, "Mary had a little lamb." You could say that he was the first to record hip-hop music.

In 1879, while working with former slave and inventor, Lewis Latimer, the two developed not the light bulb as many first believed, but the carbonized filament, which improved the vacuum inside the globe of the light bulb, resulting in a long-lasting source of light. The idea of electric lighting was not new and a number of scientists had worked on similar projects with limited success. Prior to 1879, no one had been successful in producing a long-lasting bulb, one that could be used in the home.

During the process of this discovery, Edison and Latimer developed seven elements that were essential to the practical application of electric lights use. Those elements included:

- a parallel circuit,

From Modern Times to Ancient Times

- a durable light bulb,
- an improved dynamo,
- an underground conductor network,
- devices for maintaining constant voltage,
- safety fuses and insulating materials, and
- Light sockets with on-off switches.

During his lifetime, Edison produced over 1,000 inventions including the motion picture projector. The origin of every light switch, every CD player, and every movie theater in the world can be traced to the young boy who started exploring the world of science at the age of twelve. Thomas Edison, also known as the "father of the electrical industry" was born on February 11, 1847, in Milan, Ohio, and died on October 18, 1931, in West Orange, New Jersey. The entertainment industry and the world at large, would be radically different had this inquisitive little boy, who lost most of his hearing, decided to give up on his dream.

Motivated

Your kicking me,
Is boosting me.
You are knocking me upstairs.
But this you do not seem to see,
Is helping my affairs.
You see I'm like a rubber ball,
Each knock takes me up higher.
No knock will ever make me fall,
Or whine or be a crier.

Author Unknown
(Quoted by Dr. Martin Luther King Jr.)

Dr. George Washington Carver

The sickly homeless slave boy who provided healing for our plants and solutions for our farmers

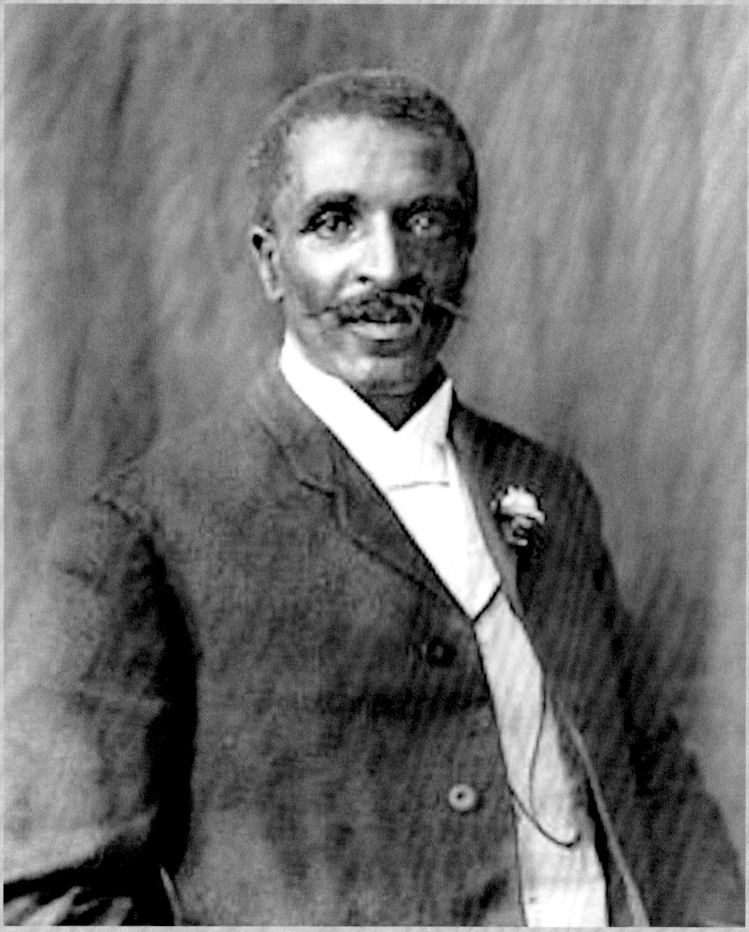

From Modern Times to Ancient Times

Long before he declined job offers from both Thomas Edison and Henry Ford. Long before he attended Simpson College, long before he developed a multitude of products from peanuts, sweet potatoes, and soy beans, and long before he walked into the agricultural laboratories of Iowa State College, young George had established a "secret garden," (a natural laboratory) in the woods near his home. In his book, George Washington Carver: an American Biography, author Rackham Holt tells his readers about the boy that neighbors called, *"the Plant Doctor."*

> "The neighbors knew the child had a magic way of growing things. They called him the "Plant Doctor," and he made house-to-house calls in Diamond Grove to prescribe for ailing plants; sometimes the cuttings wouldn't root, some were wilting, some drying, and he would recommend more or less water, or more sun. If they were seriously ill he carried them away to his secret garden. It was far enough off and hidden by bushes and nobody knew about it but himself. There he would prune or knock out the soil and shift until he had nursed them back to health and bloom. He never lost a plant in his sanatorium...."
>
> "It was in the nature of this boy to cherish his plants in solitude and, besides, Aunt Sue Carver would not allow him to bring his trash into the house. Sometimes he smuggled in a fistful of flowers or grass or even a few heads of oats, going to bed with them gripped in his hands and waking in the

morning still clutching the withered remains....
(pp. 5-6)."

This boy genius with a high-pitched falsetto voice, who stammered when he talked, was a sickly child. His sickness can be traced back to the time when he and his siblings were kidnapped and left for dead in the fields, by a cruel slave owner. Adopted and raised by the Carvers (German immigrants), little George was too sickly and too frail to work in the fields, so he was assigned household chores. In his spare time and after playing marbles and other games with the boys in the neighborhood, he would steal away to his secret laboratory in the woods.

As a child, he took on a number of odd jobs and when he had raised enough money, he would use the money to pay for his schooling. When his funds were depleted, he found other employment to continue his education. One afternoon, while working for a colored blacksmith near the town's courthouse, he noticed that a large angry white crowd had gathered outside the jail. As he watched, George said, the angry mob *"took a Negro prisoner from the jail-house and after beating out his brains, they snatched bits of souvenirs from his body, then dragged his bloody body to the public square, where they poured oil over it and set it afire."* These types of sadistic killings of blacks in the South were very common during slavery, and they continued through the 1970's. The image of a man burning to death while an angry white mob stood by resulted in many sleepless nights. George wanted to get away. At the age of ten, with the blessing of his adopted family, he left home to attend school in Neosho, Missouri.

From Modern Times to Ancient Times

His eight mile journey on barefoot brought him to the barn of Aunt Mariah and Andrew Watkins. Without seeking their permission, he made himself a bed among the hay, and slept throughout the night. In the morning, hungry and tired from his journey, he made his way to the small farm-house adjacent to the barn. There he met the child-less couple who took him in as their foster child. Unlike the Carvers, the Watkins were very religious. Aunt Mariah (as she would be called) prayed a great deal and instilled in her new foster son her devotion to the "Word of God" (Bible). When George was nearly eighty years old, he was still reading the Bible that she had given him and used as a bookmark, a special item that he embroidered under her tutelage.

Just a stone's-throw away from the Watkins' home was Lincoln School, a 14x12 one room schoolhouse with hard-wood benches, and 75 students. This was the beginnings of George's formal education. Young George was an excellent student, excelling in every subject, and had an insatiable appetite for knowledge. After completing classes in the small town of Neosho, he applied and was accepted at Highland University. As family and friends from his local church gathered at his home to wish him well, George said, "They sang hymns and prayed for his health and his Christian faith."

Later that week, he arrived at Highland, only to be told that "they did not accept Negroes." Dejected, but determine, young George found odd jobs as he traveled from one town to the next, and continued to study on his own. When he arrived in Winterset, Iowa (near Des Moines), he was taken in by Dr. and Mrs. Milholland who were members of the local Methodist Church. It was Mrs. Milholland who encouraged George to continue his education and suggested that he apply for admission at Simpson College, a Methodist college in Indianola, Iowa. Applied and accepted, George was an outstanding student and proved to have a natural talent for art. Impressed by his artistic talents and his love for plants and flowers, his art instructor (Miss Budd) used her influence to help George gain admission into Iowa Agricultural College (IAC). Convincing the college to take George as a student was a simple task. Miss Budd's father, Professor J.L. Budd, happened to be the chair of the Department of Horticulture for IAC. Excelling in geology, botany, chemistry, bacteriology, zoology, entomology and other science-related classes, this former slave boy continued his studies until he obtained a Master's Degree from Iowa State College.

By the time his life ended on January 5, 1943, this brilliant scholar, musician, singer, artist and scientist, who turned down lucrative job offers from Thomas Edison and Henry Ford, had developed over three hundred products from peanuts, a hundred products from sweet potatoes and countless products from the soy bean plant including fuel and fiberglass-type materials used in today's car manufacturing industry. Many agricultural experts and scientists from around the world often sought his counsel to solve pressing agricultural problems in their countries. The United States Department of Agriculture recognized

From Modern Times to Ancient Times

Professor Carver as "an authority on soils and plant life" and referred to him as "an unfailing and strictly accurate source of information." And it all started when he was just a child.

Carver was quoted as saying:

> "The secret to my success is found in the Bible: 'In all thy ways acknowledge Him and He shall direct thy path.'" "No books ever go into my laboratory. The thing I am to do and the way of doing it are revealed to me. I never grope for methods. The method is revealed to me the moment I am inspired to create something new. Without God to draw aside the curtain, I would be helpless".

When asked why he chose not to capitalize on all of his patents and discoveries by selling them, he quietly said: "God gave them to me. How can I sell them to someone else for profit?" Shortly before he died, he donated his entire life savings to his foundation to further his work. The sickly little slave boy from the south who never knew his real parents, will always be known as the man who single-handedly revolutionized the farming industry in America and throughout the world.

Be Kind

Scorn not the one,
Who is down today,
But cheer them in their sorrow.
For this ole world,
Is a funny ole world,
And you may be down tomorrow.

Author Unknown

Florence Nightingale

The caring teenager from a wealthy family who invested in the health of others

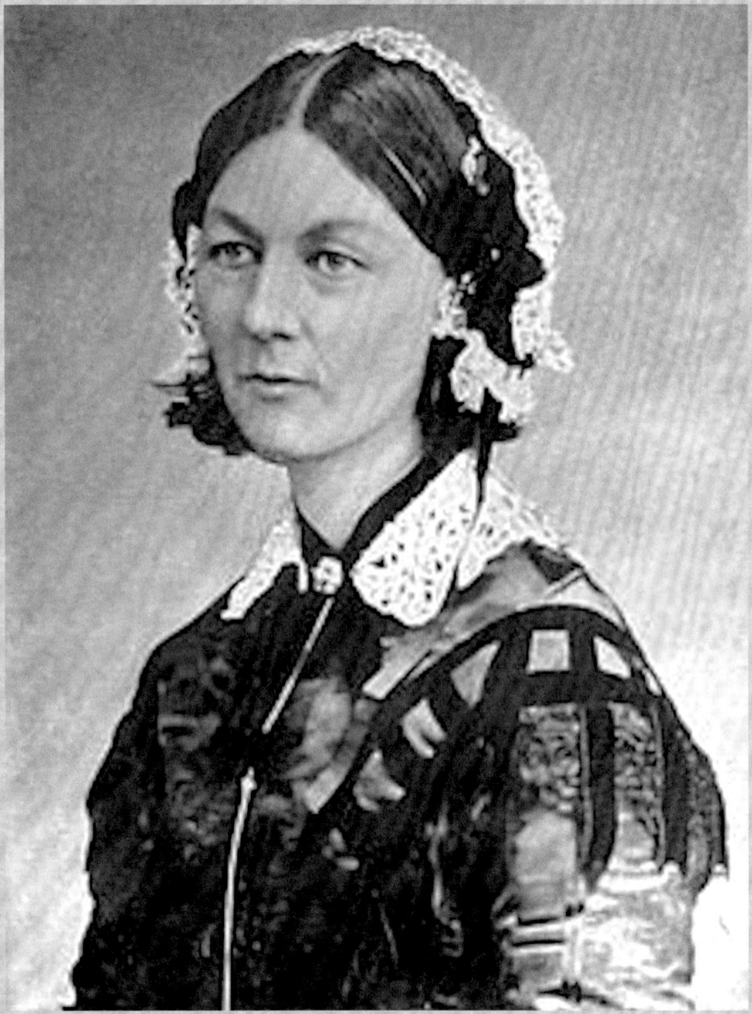

From Modern Times to Ancient Times

Determined to do something worthwhile in life, young Florence respectfully rejected her parents' plans to make her a socialite, living the British life of luxury, a lifestyle that included extravagant functions and outings for the privileged few. Florence instead chose to spend her time ministering to sick farmers on her father's estate and providing food, clothing and other necessities to those who were considered peasants in her society. Her concerns for others included both the young and the old. It was Florence who took the time to nurse her ailing grandmother back to health and she began this journey before she reached the age of twelve.

On February 7, 1837, at the age seventeen, Florence Nightingale said she heard the voice of God, telling her that He had "a special mission for her." Convinced that her calling would involve the sick and afflicted, she secretly collected a variety of medical books and spent every waking moment studying the healing profession. When she wasn't studying, she visited hospitals in London and the surrounding communities, and she did so over the strong objections of her wealthy family who (like Bill Gates' father) felt she should have better use for her time.

Florence was very close to her father. It was he who taught her Greek, Latin, French, German, Italian, mathematics, history, and philosophy. After many conversations with her dad, she finally convinced him to let her go to the Kaiserwerth (KI zer wirth) Hospital in Germany to study medicine (being away from home would also mean that she would not be around to embarrass her family with her servant-type activities). Florence was an excellent student. After graduation, she returned to London and resumed her nursing responsibilities at the local hospital.

When the Crimean War broke out in 1854, she volunteered and went to the battlefield in Scutari, Turkey to supervise thirty-eight nurses and to care for the injured. The hospital was huge, the barracks were unsanitary and the medical supplies were few. When she arrived she found a filthy facility infested with rats, fleas, and frustrated doctors who were hostile. Furniture, clothing, and bedding were deficient, "and in the corridors men laid on straw pallasses amidst filth caused by inadequate sanitation." With 200 scrub brushes, she and her fellow nurses worked relentlessly to sanitize the facility and clean the patients' clothing.

For medical supplies, some say she took as much as $100,000 of her own money to purchase what was needed. As she walked through the halls of the hospital carrying a lantern to care for the sick, she became known as the *"Lady with the Lamp"* and the *"Ministering Angel."* While saving the lives of several thousand soldiers she became ill, but she pressed on and continued to care for the injured. When the last patient left the hospital, she returned to England.

In 1860, Florence started the Nightingale School for Nurses. She will be remembered as a pioneer in the field of nursing, a reformer of hospital sanitation methods, and the one who worked most of her life to bring respect to this much-needed profession. What Florence accomplished was amazing, not because of her selfless service for others, but because most Victorian young women of that time did not

From Modern Times to Ancient Times

attend universities or pursue professional careers, particularly service oriented careers and those dominated by men.

Every doctor and every patient in the world owe a great deal of gratitude to the seventeen-year-old girl whom many referred to as the *"Ministering Angel"* and the *"Mother of the Nursing Profession."* A young girl who believed that she was called by God to care for the sick and one who chose the healing profession over a husband and remained committed to it, until the day she died (August 13, 1910, age ninety).

Wolfgang Amadeus Mozart

The child entertainer who
worked himself to death while his
music lives on

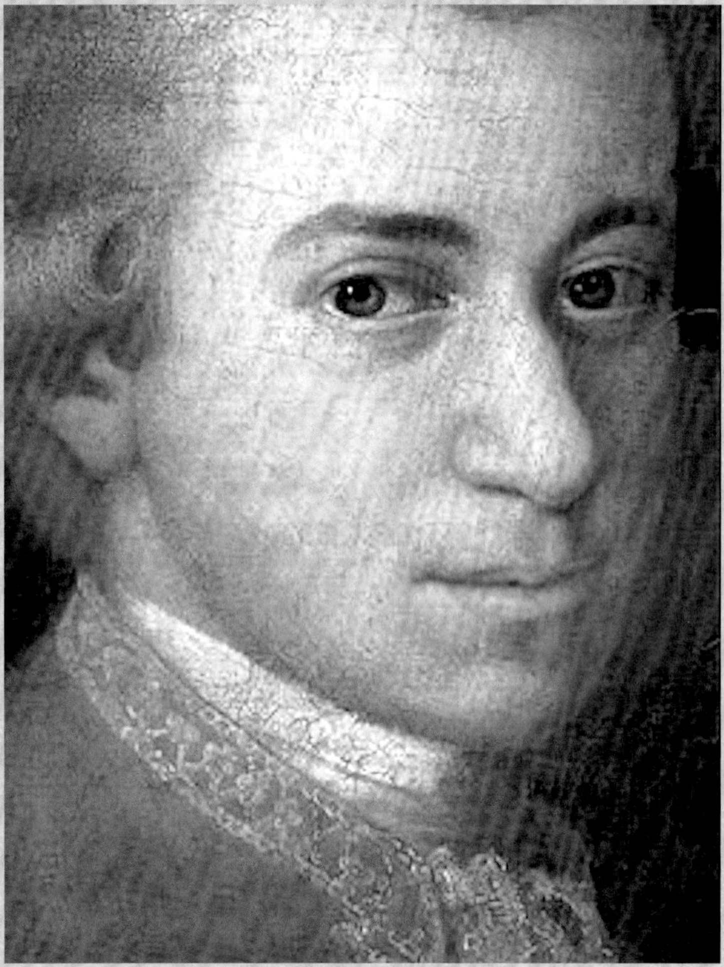

From Modern Times to Ancient Times

This amazing child composed his first piece, a clavier concerto, when he was only five years old. His father was so impressed with his son's talent that he took Wolfgang and his sister, Maria Anna, to the city of Munich where they performed for famous noblemen. Although his sister was an outstanding singer, little Mozart took the show with his skillful performance on the violin. The audience was so amazed and delighted with the five-year-old violinist that he received one encore after another. They referred to the young musician as the "little wonder-child," but his deeply religious father (of the Christian faith) knew him as a "miracle child," gifted by God.

When word of his talent reached cities throughout Europe, he was invited to play in many of the finest concert halls in the region. One of the most memorable performances was in Austria before Empress Maria Theresa. During the concert, when young Mozart tripped and fell, a beautiful little princess (Maria Antoinette) rushed over to help him. Impressed by her gesture of kindness, Wolfgang asked her to marry him, causing the crowd to burst into laughter (the two were just children - neither had reached the age of seven). When he offered the marriage proposal, little did he know that one day this beautiful little girl would become the Queen of France. The seven-year-old prodigy regained his composure, completed four sonatas, and continued to woo audiences all over Europe.

The "wonder-child," (Wolfgang Amadeus Mozart), was born into a family of musicians in 1756. His father, Leopold, was a great composer and his sister Maria Anna was a talented singer. As time went on, Mozart mastered the piano and the violin and became a great composer. His life's works included writing operas and composing music for orchestras, singers and chamber groups. While on tour, he devoted every idle moment to composing music, many times working without sleep. By the time he was twenty-one, he had completed almost three hundred works. By twenty-nine, he had completed several operas, including the famous "Marriage of Figaro" and by thirty-five, he had literally worked himself to death. Like many young entertainers and professional athletes today, Mozart earned a great deal of money. However, he spent it as fast as he made it. From time to time he was deeply in debt, which forced him to teach, give concerts, and furiously compose one piece of music after another to keep from going bankrupt.

 Fellow composer, Joseph Haydn referred to Mozart as "the greatest composer I know." Today the "wonder boy," or as his father would say, "the miracle child's" music continues to bring joy to millions around the world in capacity-filled symphony halls.

Leonardo da Vinci

The illegitimate child of a young peasant girl who produced beauty with a brush

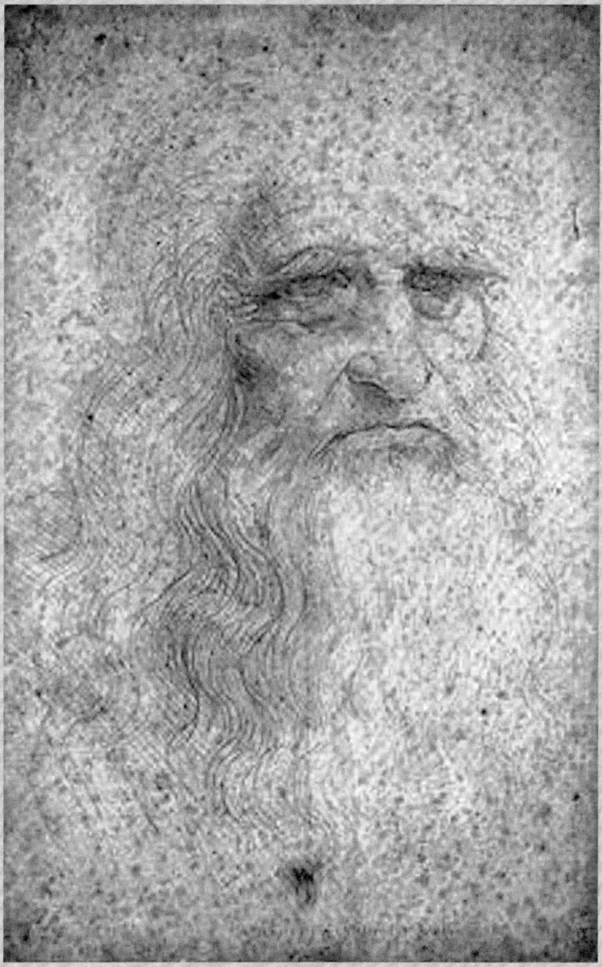

From Modern Times to Ancient Times

His misfortune of being the illegitimate son of a young peasant girl, was offset by being fortunate enough to be born into a family of skillful artists. Leonardo da Vinci was born on April 15, 1452, in the small town of Vinci, Italy, forty years before Columbus discovered the Americas. When his father took custody of his son at birth, the biological mother moved to a neighboring town, married and started a new family. The two separate parents continued to have children, providing young Leonardo with seventeen half brothers and sisters.

Leonardo, who would be eventually known as a master painter, sculptor, scientist, inventor, architect, mathematician, and philosopher, grew up in a family that had a longstanding tradition in the field of art. At an early age, Leonardo exhibited many extraordinary talents in a variety of areas, including music and illustrations. It is said that as a young student he was so brilliant that he confused his math teachers with a barrage of thought-provoking questions.

When he turned fifteen, his father apprenticed him to the renowned workshop of Andrea del Verrocchio in Florence. Verrocchio was one of Italy's finest painters. During the first stages of Leonardo apprenticeship, Verrocchio assigned the young student to common jobs ranging from preparing materials for their projects to actually assisting with some of the painting. The fifteen-year-old apprentice's talents were so impressive that even his mentor was astonished, particularly when Verrocchio's gave him an assignment to paint an angel in the "The Baptism of Christ." Legend has it that Leonardo's painting was so much better than his master's that Verrocchio allegedly resolved, "never to paint again." Art critics say, Verrocchio recognized that he would never be able to match this young man's talents so he gave up painting and concentrated on sculptures.

As a child, Leonardo also developed a unique interest in machines. He determined that if he could ascertain how each separate machine part worked, he could easily modify them to improve their efficiency, or he could create new inventions from their basic make-up. With the combined talents of illustrating, writing and mechanical aptitude, he set out to write and illustrate the first systematic explanation of how machines work and how the various components of the machines could be combined. Leonardo da Vinci was a young genius with a keen eye and an incredible mind. With these God-given talents he designed advanced military weapons and made important scientific discoveries that were far ahead of his own time. The sketches that he left behind revealed that he had an advanced conceptual knowledge of helicopters, military tanks, solar power and calculators. The fifteen-year-old apprentice whose artistic talents far exceeded his mentor's, died fifty-two years later at the age of sixty-seven, in 1519.

Da Vinci was a true master artist and will always be known for his famous paintings of *The Last Supper* (1495-97), *The Mona Lisa* (1503-06), *The Adoration of the Magi* (1481-82), *Lady with an Ermine* (1483-90), *Madonna Litta* (1490-91) and *Virgin of the Rocks* (1502-06).

Millions today still enjoy the works of the young man who began his career at the age of fifteen.

Mother Teresa

The teenager who provided compassion for the poor and healing for the sick and afflicted

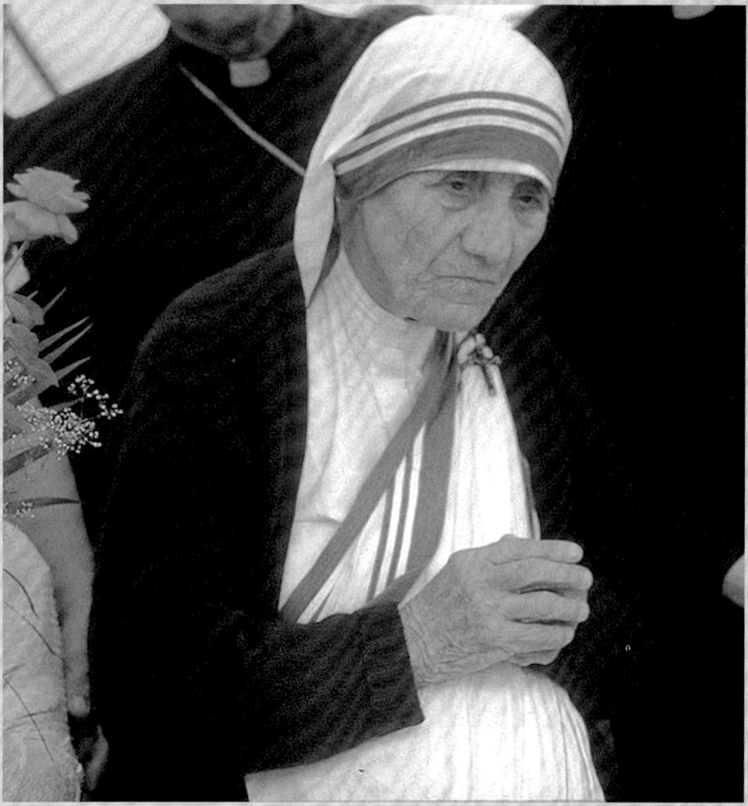

From Modern Times to Ancient Times

She received her first communion at the age of five and a half, she was confirmed at the age of six and by the age of twelve, she knew that she was born to do something special for God and mankind. But little did she know that her mission would span to the four corners of the earth, covering the former Soviet Union, Asia, Africa, Latin America and Eastern Europe; and that it would involve a multitude of charities that would provide aid to the poorest of the poor and relief to millions who were victims of natural disasters (i.e. floods, epidemics, and famine). The young lady's work would eventually establish over 500 "missions of compassion" in North America, Europe, and Australia, where the care for shut-ins, alcoholics, homeless, and AIDS patients would be provided by over one million co-workers in more than 100 countries.

She was born Agnes Gonxha Bojaxhiu in Skopje, Macedonia, in the former Yugoslavia on August 27, 1910. She was the youngest of three children. She was raised in a spiritual home of compassion. Her mother, Drana, was known for helping the underprivileged, and for always having money, food and medicine for the poor. Drana would tell her children, that the needy were part of the human family and it was their responsibility to help them. When the poor wouldn't come to the Bojaxhiu home, mother Drana would take meals and medicine to their homes, often accompanied by young Agnes.

Resources for the poor would soon come to an end when Agnes' father died of internal bleeding at the age of forty-five. With few resources and an entrepreneurial spirit,

Teens and Young People Who Impacted the World

Agnes's mother started a hand embroidery business and later became a design consultant for the owners of a local textile factory. As the family's financial status improved, they resumed their compassionate services to the poor.

As a teenager, Agnes became a member of a youth group, called, "sodality," in her local parish. Through her involvement, she became interested in becoming a missionary. At the age of eighteen (1928) she left home to join the institute of the Blessed Virgin Mary, known as the Sisters of Loreto in Ireland. There she received the name Sister Mary Teresa after St. Therese of Lisieux.

One year later, at the age nineteen, she arrived in Calcutta, India and established an unprecedented legacy of compassion by opening schools, orphanages and homes in the slums to care for the needy. After arriving there, she found men, women, and children dying on the streets because they had been rejected by local hospitals. Their rejection motivated the young servant to learn basic medicine. After her medical training she would often go from house to house treating the sick and afflicted. To have a place to care for those who would otherwise be "condemned to die in the gutter," she and her co-workers rented a room to meet this need. It is reported that one day Mother Teresa found a woman "half eaten by maggots and rats" lying in front of a Calcutta hospital. She sat with the woman until she died. In 1982, at the height of the conflict in Beirut, Lebanon, the then frail nun rescued thirty-seven children trapped in a frontline hospital by brokering a temporary cease-fire between the Israeli army and the Palestinian guerillas.

The twelve-year-old girl who felt that God wanted her to touch the lives of others is now known as one of the greatest humanitarians of modern times. Her work has been recognized and acclaimed throughout the world, receiving a multitude of awards and distinctions, including the Pope John XXIII's Peace Prize (1971) and the Nehru Prize for promoting international peace and understanding (1972). She also received the prestigious Balzan Prize (1979) and the Templeton and Magsaysay awards.

In 1979, when she received the Nobel Peace, she said,

"I choose the poverty of our poor people. But I am grateful to receive (the Nobel) in the name of the hungry, the naked, the homeless, of the crippled, of the blind, of the lepers, of all those people who feel unwanted, unloved, and uncared-for throughout society, people that have become a burden to the society and are shunned by everyone."

On October 19, 2003, Pope John Paul II beatified Mother Teresa before a cheering crowd of over 300,000 who had gathered in Saint Peter's Square for the celebration. The crowd represented and reflected the diversity of the world that she had touched with her life of kindness and compassion. Mother Teresa, the nineteen year old guardian angel who had dedicated her life to ministering to the sick and afflicted, died at the age of eighty-seven (1997), after battling with her own sickness during the final years of her life.

Jesus Inspiring Good in Others

A pre-teen filled with love
for others

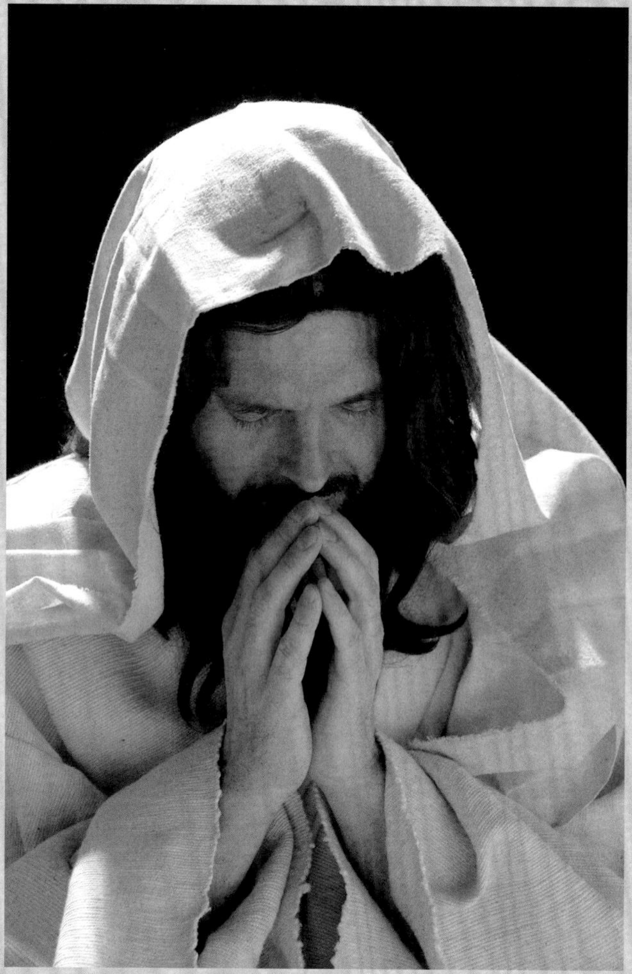

From Modern Times to Ancient Times

In America, most public school students are first introduced to this historical figure while studying the Roman/Julian calendar and the meanings of AD, BC, and BCE. Others are introduced to him in Sunday school classes as part of the Christmas story. Few realize that it wasn't the fact that He was born in a manger in the town of Bethlehem that brought him fame. It was His teachings and His acts of compassion that inspired others to do the same is what makes Him so special. Jesus, the young boy who started his mission in life at the age of twelve, impacted our society in more ways than we can ever imagine. It was He who inspired:

- Florence Nightingale to care for the sick.
- Mother Teresa to comfort the poor.
- The Abolitionist Movement to end slavery.
- Dr. Martin Luther King Jr. to fight for social justice.
- Father Flanagan to start Boys Town.
- Jean Henri Dunant to form the Red Cross.
- William Booth to start the Salvation Army.
- Levi Coffin to create the Underground Railroad.
- Christian Missionaries to establish our Historically Black Colleges.
- Christian Educators to start our Ivy League Colleges.

Teens and Young People Who Impacted the World

- The Founding Fathers to include religious freedom in the First Amendment of our Constitution, and to include the words "created equal" and "Inalienable Rights" in our Declaration of Independence.

He was only twelve years old (not thirty), when he first started challenging the same powerful people who would later call for His death. The Scripture places Him in the temple conversing with the scholarly men of his day at the age of twelve. The Bible says, "All that heard him were astonished at his understanding and answers" (Luke 2:47 - KJV). The Scripture implies that even at a very young age, He was able to hold His own and confound the wise as He would do throughout the rest of His life (Luke 2:52 KJV).

It was Jesus who coined the phrase to "do unto others as you would have them to do unto you;" and it was He who told the world to "love your neighbor as yourself" (Matthew 7:12, Luke 10: 27-28 KJV). During His lifetime He never endorsed wars, never endorsed civil disobedience and never encouraged revenge. Because loving, caring and compassion were always a part of His message and mission, many refer to His birth, life, and death as the "greatest love story ever told."

From His story of the Good Samaritan, we have adopted the concept of being "neighborly" by serving others. The story of the Good Samaritan as told in St. Luke 10:25-37, involved a man of one ethnicity going out of his way to help an injured person of another ethnicity, simple because the person was in need. From this story we get what is known as our "Good Samaritan Laws." These laws

From Modern Times to Ancient Times

were designed to protect those individuals who go out of their way to help others who are injured or ill, without fear of being sued for mistakes that may occur during that process. These laws are intended to reduce bystanders' hesitation to assist others for fear of being prosecuted for unintentional injury or wrongful death. The United Good Neighbor Fund (known today as United Way) was also a modern-day expression of the Good Samaritan story and Jesus' commandment to *"Love our neighbors as ourselves."*

The Scripture records that His acts of compassion included:

1. Feeding the hungry,
2. healing the sick,
3. receiving the outcast,
4. delivering the captive and
5. helping those with career and financial problems.

Then he told his followers, *"Greater work than these will you do"* (St John 14:12), and they have. From His birth to His death, His life has been an inspiration to millions of individuals who created a multitude of social services and health organizations to represent the Christ-like lifestyle that He demonstrated during His lifetime. Many who follow Him believe that He is best honored by *'the life that we live and the service that we give."*

In addition to inspiring billions, His acts of compassion are emulated through a multitude of different Christian organizations and denominations that have started tens of thousands of hospitals, clinics, rest homes, and retirement homes (world-wide), many under the auspices of Catholic, Presbyterian, Lutheran, Methodist, Baptist, Seventh-Day Adventist, Pentecostal, Mormon and other churches. In His name, literally millions of other charities and food banks were started to help the poor and the outcast both here in America and throughout the world, simply because He taught that when you have neglected the poor and the rejects of our society, you have rejected and neglected "Me" (Matthew 25:40).

With rare exceptions, every credit card transaction, every student's homework assignment, every birthdate and every legal document in the civilized world, references His life and death in dates of AD and BC and, despite the fact that some have exploited His name to justify their ungodly acts and evil deeds; wars were stopped temporarily to honor Him, holidays were created to remember Him, and billions of lives have been blessed because of Him; and it all started 2,000 years ago when the twelve- year-old boy told His mother that it was time for Him to *"be about His father's business"* (Luke 2:49 KJV).

Mary – Jesus's Teenage Mother

The committed teenage mother & wife

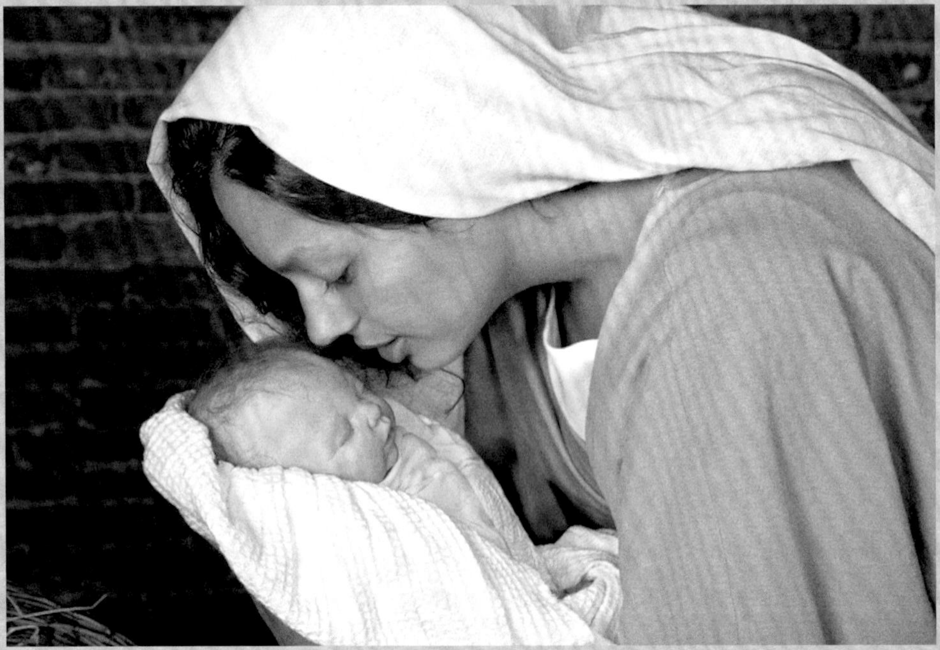

From Modern Times to Ancient Times

Christmas is never complete without the story of Bethlehem where Mary, the mother of Jesus, gives birth to a baby boy and wraps Him in swaddling clothes and lays Him in a manger. But what is not told, is that most scholars today believe that Mary was just sixteen or seventeen years old when she gave birth to Jesus, thus making her the most famous teenage mother in world history; and after the death of her husband Joseph, one might say she became the most famous single parent of all times. Unlike the women of our day, women of ancient cultures married and gave birth at a very young age. According to Jewish scholars, Jewish tradition teaches that a mature Jewish girl had the right to give herself in marriage if she was *"more than twelve and a half years of age."*

    The Bible refers to Mary as a *"virgin,"* meaning a woman who had not engaged in sexual intercourse. In the Bible, "virgins" usually refers to the younger women, and such was the case of Mary who was engaged to be married to Joseph. Today, many religious organizations (such as the Catholic faith) and millions of other individuals honor this special young mother who was *"highly favored"* by God, according to the Bible.

    Selecting a young teenage girl, to be the mother of the greatest leader of humanitarianism that ever lived (Jesus), says a lot about God and His thoughts and respect for teenagers. It is not surprising that He would select Mary, considering the fact that throughout the Bible you will find that God consistently chose many younger persons over older persons to carry out His mission. Among those chosen are

Teens and Young People Who Impacted the World

Esther, David, Daniel, Samuel, Solomon, Joseph, Samson, and Jeremiah to name a few and perhaps even Adam and Eve. Bible references of the young life of Jesus, Mary, and other young Jewish leaders can be found in Appendix III.

Advice to Young Women

By

Gale Baker Stanton

IF

If you can trust yourself though others doubt you
And conquer fears that limit what you dare
So you can freely give to those about you
The skills and talents that are yours to share;

If you can live, not for your pleasure only,
But gladly lend your gentleness and grace
To warm the hearts of those whose lives are lonely
And help to make their world a better place;

If you can balance dreams with practicality
And deal in facts, but never lose ideals,
If you can face the harshness of reality
And find the truths that prejudice conceals;

Teens and Young People Who Impacted the World

If you can be courageous when defeated
And humble in the face of victory,
Or give your best until a task's completed,
However difficult that task may be;

If you can temper facts with understanding
And seek to gently guide, not to control,
And neither be too lax nor too demanding,
But keep in mind the worth of every soul…

If you can strive, not caring who gets credit,
And work at building bridges, and not walls,
Or hearing idle slander, just forget it
And never fail to help someone who falls;

If you can give your help without begrudging
The patience, time and effort you impart,
Or look at others' weakness without judging
And see, not with your eyes, but with your heart;

If you can take resources that surround you
And use them in the way you feel you should,
You'll be a woman…and all those around you
Will be the richer for your womanhood!

Advice for Young Men

By
Rudyard Kipling

IF

If you can keep your head when all about you
Are losing theirs and blaming it on you,
If you can trust yourself when all men doubt you,
But make allowance for their doubting too;
If you can wait and not be tired by waiting,
Or being lied about, don't deal in lies,
Or being hated, don't give way to hating,
And yet don't look too good, nor talk too wise:

If you can dream - and not make dreams your master,
If you can think - and not make thoughts your aim;
If you can meet with Triumph and Disaster
And treat those two impostors just the same;
If you can bear to hear the truth you've spoken
Twisted by knaves to make a trap for fools,
Or watch the things you gave your life to, broken,
And stoop and build 'em up with worn-out tools:

Teens and Young People Who Impacted the World

If you can make one heap of all your winnings
And risk it all on one turn of pitch-and-toss,
And lose, and start again at your beginnings
And never breathe a word about your loss;
If you can force your heart and nerve and sinew
To serve your turn long after they are gone,
And so hold on when there is nothing in you
Except the Will which says to them: "Hold on!"

If you can talk with crowds and keep your virtue,
Or walk with kings - nor lose the common touch,
If neither foes nor loving friends can hurt you,
If all men count with you, but none too much;
If you can fill the unforgiving minute
With sixty seconds' worth of distance run,
Yours is the Earth and everything that's in it,
And - which is more - you'll be a Man, my son!

      Rudyard Kipling (1865-1936)

APPENDIX I

Court's Decision in Browder *vs* Gayle

JUDGMENT:

This cause came on to be heard before three-judge court, duly convened pursuant to the provision of Title 28, United States Code, Sections, 2281 and 2284.

"After trial on the merits and careful consideration of the evidence therein adduced and after oral arguments and submission of briefs by all parties, the Court being fully advised in the promises, found in an opinion handed down on June 5, 1956, that the enforced segregation of Negro and white passengers on motor buses operating in the City of Montgomery as required by Section 301 (31a, 31b and 31c) of Title 48, Code of Alabama, 1940, as amended, and Sections 10 and 11 of Chapter 6 of the Code of the City of Montgomery, 1952, violates the Constitution and the laws of the United States.

Teens and Young People Who Impacted the World

Now in accordance with that opinion, Adjudged and Decreed that Section 301 (31a, 31b and 31c) of Title 28, Code of Alabama, 1940, as amended, and Sections, 10 and 11 of Chapter 6 of the Code of the City of Montgomery, 1952, are unconstitutional and void in that they deny and deprive plaintiffs [which includes Ms. Claudette Colvin] *and other Negro citizens similarly situated of the equal protection of the laws and due process of law secured by the Fourteenth Amendment of the Constitution of the United States and rights and privileges secured by Title 42, United States Code, Sections 1981 and 1983.*

It is furthered Ordered, Adjudged and Decreed that the defendants, their successors in office, assigns, agents, servants, employees, and persons acting on their behalf, be and they are hereby permanently enjoined and restrained from enforcing the aforesaid statutes and ordinances or any other statutes or ordinances which may require plaintiffs or any other negroes similarly situated to submit to segregation in the bus transportational facilities in the City of Montgomery, from doing any acts or taking any action to require the Montgomery Bus Lines, Inc., or its drivers, or any, other public bus transportation facility, or its drivers, to enforces such statutes or ordinances requiring the segregation of white and Negro passengers in the operation of public motor bus transportation facilities in the city of Montgomery…"(Browder v. Gayle, June 19, 1956)"

APPENDIX II

Democratic Governors of the Jim Crow South from 1877 to 1977

B.B. Comer
1907-1911

Emmet O'Neal
1911-1915

Charles Henderson
1915-1919

Thomas Kilby
1919-1923

William W. Brandon
1923-1927

Bibb Graves
1927-1931

Benjamin M. Miller
1931-1935

Bibb Graves
1935-1939

Frank M. Dixon
1939-1943

Chauncey Sparks
1943-1947

James E. Folsom Sr.
1947-1951

Gordon Persons
1951-1959

Teens and Young People Who Impacted the World

James E. Folsom Sr.
1955-1959

John Patterson
1959-1963

George Wallace
1963-1967

Lurleen Wallace
1967-1968

Albert Brewer
1968-1971

George Wallace
1971-1987

ARKANSAS

Augustus H. Garland
1874-1877

William R. Miller
1877-1881

Thomas J. Churchill
1881-1883

James H. Berry
1883-1885

Simon P. Hughes Jr.
1885-1889

James P. Eagle
1889-1893

William M. Fishback
1893-1895

James P. Clarke
1895-1897

Daniel W. Jones
1897-1901

Jeff Davis
1901-1907

John S. Little
1907-1907

John I. Moore
1907-1907

Xenophon O. Pindall
1907-1909

From Modern Times to Ancient Times

Jesse M. Martin
1909-1909

George W. Donaghey
1909-1913

Joseph T. Robinson
1913-1913

Junius M. Futrell
1913-1913

George W. Hays
1913-1917

Charles H. Brough
1917-1921

Tomas C. McRae
1921-1925

Tom J. Terral
1925-1927

John E. Martineau
1927-1928

Harvey Parnell
1928-1933

Junius M. Futrell
1933-1937

Carl E. Bailey
1937-1941

Hommer M. Adkins
1941-1945

Benjamin T. Laney
1945-1949

Sid McMath
1949-1953

Francis Cherry
1953-1955

Orval Faubus
1955-1967

Dale Bumpers
1971-1975

Bob C. Riley
1975-1975

David Pryor
1975-1979

Teens and Young People Who Impacted the World

FLORIDA

George F. Drew
1877-1881

William D. Bloxham
1881-1885

Edward A. Perry
1885-1889

Francis P. Fleming
1889-1893

Whenry L. Mitchell
1893-1897

William D. Bloxham
1897-1901

William S. Jennings
1901-1905

Napoleon B. Broward
1905-1909

Albert W. Gilchrist
1909-1913

Park Trammell
1913-1917

Sidney J. Catts
1917-1921

Cary A. Hardee
1921-1925

John W. Martin
1925-1929

Doyle E. Carlton
1929-1933

David Sholtz
1933-1937

Fred P. Cone
1937-1941

Spessard Holland
1941-1945

Millard F. Caldwell
1945-1949

Fuller Warren
1949-1953

From Modern Times to Ancient Times

Daniel T. McCarty
1953-1953

Charlesy E. Johns
1953-1955

LeRoy Collins
1955-1961

C. Farris Bryant
1961-1965

W. Haydon Burns
1965-1967

Claude R. Kirk Jr.
1967-1971

Reubin O'D. Askew
1971-1979

<u>GEORGIA</u>

James M. Smith
1872-1877

Alfred H. Colquitt
1877-1882

Alexander H. Stephens
1882-1883

James S. Boynton
1883-1883

Henry D. McDaniel
1883-1886

John B. Gordon
1886-1890

William J. Northen
1890-1894

William Y. Atkinson
1894-1898

Allen D. Chandler
1898-1902

Joseph Terrell
1902-1907

Hoke Smith
1907-1909

Joseph M. Brown
1909-1911

Teens and Young People Who Impacted the World

Hoke Smith 1911-1911	Eugene Talmadge 1933-1937
John M. Slaton 1911-1912	Eurith D. Rives 1937-1941
Joseph M. Brown 1912-1913	Ellis Arnall 1943-1947
John M. Slaton 1913-1915	Herman Talmadge 1947-1947
Nathaniel E. Harris 1915-1917	Melvin E. Thompson 1947-1948
Hugh M. Dorsey 1917-1921	Herman Talmadge 1948-1955
Thomas W. Harwick 1921-1923	Marvin Griffin 1955-1959
Clifford Walker 1923-1927	Ernest Vandiver 1959-1963
Lamartine G. Hardman 1927-1931	Carl E. Sanders 1963-1967
Richard Russell Jr. 1931-1933	Lester Maddox 1967-1971

From Modern Times to Ancient Times

Jimmy Carter
1971-1975

KENTUCKY

James B. McCreary
1875-1879

Luke P. Blackburn
1879-1883

J. Proctor Knott
1883-1887

Simon B. Buckner
1887-1891

John Young Brown
1891-1895

William Goebel
1900-1900

J.C.W. Beckham
1900-1907

James B. MccCreary
1911-1915

Augustus O. Stanley
1915-1919

James D. Black
1919-1919

William J. Fields
1923-1927

Ruby Laffoon
1931-1935

A.B. Happy Chandler
1935-1939

Keen Johnson
1939-1943

Earle . Clements
1947-1950

Lawrence W. Wetherby
1950-1955

A.B. Happy Chandler
1955-1959

Bert T. Combs
1959-1963

Teens and Young People Who Impacted the World

Edward T. Breathitt
1963-1967

Wendell H. Ford
1971-1974

Julian M. Carroll
1974-1979

LOUISIANA

Francis T. Nicholls
1877-1880

Louis A. Wiltz
1880-1881

Samuel D. McEnery
1881-1888

Francis T. Nicholls
1888-1892

Murphy J. Foster
1892-1900

William W. Heard
1900-1904

Newton C. Blanchard
1904-1908

Jared Y. Sanders Sr.
1908-1912

Luther E. Hall
1912-1916

Ruffin G. Pleasant
1916-1920

John M. Parker
1920-1924

Henry L. Fuqua
1924-1926

Oramel H. Simpson
1926-1928

Huey Pierce Long
1928-1932

Alvin Olin King
1932-1932

Oscar Kelly Allen
1932-1936

From Modern Times to Ancient Times

James A. Noe
1936-1936

Richard W. Leche
1936-1939

Earl K. Long
1939-1940

Sam H. Jones
1940-1944

Jimmie H. Davis
1944-1948

Earl K. Long
1948-1952

Robert F. Kennon
1952-1956

Earl K. Long
1956-1960

Jimmie H. Davis
1960-1964

John J. McKeithen
1964-1972

Edwin W. Edwards
1972-1980

MISSISSIPPI

John Marshall Stone
1876-1882

Robert Lowry
1882-1890

John Marshall Stone
1890-1896

A. J. McLaurin
1896-1900

Andrew H. Longino
1900-1904

James K. Vardaman
1904-1908

Edmund F. Noel
1908-1912

Earl Brewer
1912-1916

Teens and Young People Who Impacted the World

Theodore G. Bilbo
1916-1920

Lee M. Russell
1920-1924

Henry L. Whitfield
1924-1927

H. Dennis Murphree
1927-1928

Theodor G. Bilbo
1928-1932

Sennett Conner
1932-1936

Hugh L. White
1936-1940

Paul B. Johnson
1940-1943

Dennis Murphree
1943-1944

Thomas Bailey
1944-1946

Fielding L. Wright
1946-1952

Hugh L. White
1952-1956

James P. Coleman
1956-1960

Ross R. Barnett
1960-1964

Paul B. Johnson Jr.
1964-1968

John B. Willis
1968-1972

William Waller
1972-1976

Cliff Finch
1976-1980

NORTH CAROLINA

Zebulon Baird Vance
1877-1879

From Modern Times to Ancient Times

Thomas J. Jarvis
1879-1885

Alfred M. Scales
1885-1889

Daniel G. Fowle
1889-1891

Thomas M. Holt
1891-1893

Elias Carr
1893-1897

Daniel L. Russell
1897-1901

Charles B. Aycock
1901-1905

Robert B. Glenn
1905-1909

William W. Kitchin
1909-1913

Locke Craig
1913-1917

Thomas W. Bickett
1917-1921

Cameron Morrison
1921-1925

Angus W. McLean
192-1929

Olive M. Gardner
1929-1933

John C.B. Ehringhaus
1933-1937

Clyde R. Hoey
1937-1941

J. Melville Broughton
1941-1945

R. Gregg Cherry
1945-1949

W. Kerr Scott
1949-1953

William B. Umstead
1953-1954

Teens and Young People Who Impacted the World

Luther H. Hodges
1954-1961

Terry Sanford
1961-1965

Dan K. Moore
1965-1969

Robert W. Scott
1969-1973

OKLAHOMA

William C. Renfrow
1893-1897

Charles N. Haskell
1907-1911

Lee Cruce
1911-1915

R.L. Williams
1915-1919

James B.A. Robertson
1919-1923

Jack C. Walton
1923-1923

Martin E. Trapp
1923-1927

Martin E. TrappMartine

Henry S. Johnston
1927-1929

William J. Holloway
1929-1931

William H. Murray
1931-1935

Earnest W. Marland
1935-1939

Leon C. Phillips
1939-1943

Robert S. Kerr
1943-1947

Roy J. Turner
1947-1951

From Modern Times to Ancient Times

Johnston Murray
1951-1955

Raymond D. Gary
1955-1959

J. Howard Edmond
1959-1963

George Nigh
1963-1963

David Hall
1971-1975

David L. Boren
1975-1979

<u>SOUTH CAROLINA</u>

Wade Hampton III
1876-1879

William D. Simpson
1879-1880

Thomas B. Jeter
1880-1880

Johnson Hagood
1880-1882

Hugh S. Thompson
1882-1886

John C. Sheppard
1886-1886

John P. Richardson III
1886-1890

Benjamin R. Tillman
1890-1894

John G. Evans
1894-1897

William H. Ellerbe
1897-1899

Miles B. McSweeney
1899-1903

Ducan C. Heyward
1903-1907

Martin F. Ansel
1907-1911

Teens and Young People Who Impacted the World

Coleman L. Blease 1911-1915	Joseph E. Harley 1941-1942
Charles A. Smith 1915-1915	Richard M. Jeffries 1942-1943
Richard I. Manning III 1915-1919	Olin D. Johnston 1943-1945
Robert A. Cooper 1919-1922	Ransome J. Williams 1945-1947
Wilson G. Harvey 1922-1923	Strom Thurmond 1947-1951
Thomas G. McLeod 1923-1927	James F. Byrnes 1951-1955
John G. Richards Jr. 1927-1931	George B. Timmerman Jr. 1955-1959
Ibra C. Blackwood 1931-1935	Ernest F. Hoillings 1959-1963
Olin D. Johnson 1935-1939	Donald S. Russell 1963-1965
Burnet R. Maybank 1939-1941	Robert E. McNair 1965-1971

Teens and Young People Who Impacted the World

John C. West
1971-1975

TENNESSEE

John C. Brown
1871-1875

James D. Porter Jr.
1875-1879

Albert S. Marks
1879-1881

Williams B. Bate
1883-1887

Robert L. Taylor
1887-1891

Peter Turney
1893-1897

Robert L. Taylor
1897-1899

Benton McMillin
1899-1903

James B. Frazier
1903-1905

John I. Cox
1905-1907

Malcolm R. Patterson
1907-1911

Tom . Rye
1915-1919

A.H. Roberts
1919-1921

Austin Peay
1923-1927

Henry Hollis Horton
1927-1933

Harry H. McAlister
1933-1937

Gordon Browning
1937-1939

Prentice Cooper
1939-1945

Teens and Young People Who Impacted the World

Jim N. McCord
1945-1949

Gordon Browning
1949-1953

Frank G. Clement
1953-1959

Buford Ellington
1959-1963

Frank G. Clement
1963-1967

Buford Elllington
1967-1971

Ray Blanton
1975-1979

TEXAS

Richard B. Hubbard
1876-1879

Oran M. Robert
1879-1883

John Ireland
1883-1887

Lawrence S. Ross
1887-1891

James S. Hogg
1891-1895

Charles A. Culberson
1895-1899

Joseph D. Sayers
1899-1903

S.W.T. Lanham
1903-1907

Thomas M. Campbell
1907-1911

Oscar B. Colquitt
1911-1915

James E. Ferguson
1915-1917

William P. Hobby
1917-1921

Teens and Young People Who Impacted the World

Pat M. Neff
1921-1925

Miriam A. Ferguson
1925-1927

DanMoody
1927-1931

Ross S. Sterling
1931-1933

Miriam A. Ferguson
1933-1935

James V. Allred
1935-1939

W. Lee O'Daniel
1939-1941

Coke R. Steveson
1941-1947

Beauford H. Jester
1947-1949

Allan Shivers
1949-1957

Price Daniel
1957-1963

John Connally
1963-1969

Preston Smith
1969-1973

Dolph Briscoe
1973-1979

VIRGINIA

James L. Kemper
1874-1878

Frederick W.M. Holiday
1878-1882

Fitzhugh Lee
1886-1890

Philip W. McKinney
1890-1894

Charles T. O'Ferrall
1894-1898

Teens and Young People Who Impacted the World

James H. Tyler
1898-1902

Andrew J. Montague
1902-1906

Claude A. Swanson
1906-1910

William H. Mann
1910-1914

Henry C. Stuart
1914-1918

Westmoreland Davis
1918-1822

Elbert L. Trinkle
192-1926

Harry F. Byrd
1926-1930

John G. Pollard
1930-1934

George C. Peery
1934-1938

James H. Price
1938-1942

Colgate Darden
1942-1946

William M. Tuck
1946-1950

John S. Battle
1950-1954

Thomas B. Stanley
1954-1958

James L. Almond Jr.
1958-1962

Albertis S. Harrison Jr.
1962-1966

Mills E. Godwin Jr.
1966-1970

APPENDIX III

Scripture References of Jesus, Mary & Young Jewish Leaders

Jesus Early Life -Luke 2:40-46

- There the child [Jesus] became a strong, robust lad, and was known for wisdom beyond his years; and God poured out his blessings on him.
- When Jesus was twelve years old he accompanied his parents to Jerusalem for the annual Passover Festival, which they attended each year.
- After the celebration was over they started home to Nazareth, but Jesus stayed behind in Jerusalem. His parents didn't miss him the first day,
- for they assumed he was with friends among the other travelers. But when he didn't show up that evening, they started to look for him among their relatives and friends;

- and when they couldn't find him, they went back to Jerusalem to search for him there.
- Three days later they finally discovered him. He was in the Temple, sitting among the teachers of Law, discussing deep questions with them and amazing everyone with his understanding and answers. (Luke 2:40-46 LB)

Biblical References of Jesus's Compassionate Teachings

Jesus's Teachings of The Good Samaritan & Loving Our Neighbors

- One day an expert on Moses' laws came to test Jesus' orthodoxy by asking him this question: "Teacher, what does a man need to do to live forever in heaven?"
- Jesus replied, "What does Moses' law say about it?"
- "It says," he replied, "that you must love the Lord your God with all your heart, and with all your soul, and with all your strength, and with all your mind. And you must <u>love your neighbor just as much as you love yourself</u>."
- "Right!" Jesus told him. "Do this and you shall live!"
- The man wanted to justify (his lack of love for some kinds of people), so he asked, "Which neighbors?"

From Modern Times to Ancient Times

- Jesus replied with an illustration: "A Jew going on a trip from Jerusalem to Jericho was attacked by bandits. They stripped him of his clothes and money, and beat him up and left him lying half dead beside the road.

- "By chance a Jewish priest came along; and when he saw the man lying there, he crossed to the other side of the road and passed him by.

- A Jewish Temple-assistant walked over and looked at him lying there, but then went on.

- "But a despised Samaritan came along, and when he saw him, he felt deep pity.

- Kneeling beside him the Samaritan soothed his wounds with medicine and bandaged them. Then he put the man on his donkey and walked along beside him till they came to an inn, where he nursed him through the night.

- The next day he handed the innkeeper two twenty-dollar bills and told him to take care of the man. 'If his bill runs higher than that,' he said, 'I'll pay the difference the next time I am here.'

- "Now which <u>of these three would you say was a neighbor</u> to the bandits' victim?"

- The man replied, "The one who showed him some pity." Then Jesus said, "Yes, now go and do the same." (Luke 10:25-37 LB)

Jesus Teachings of The Golden Rule

- "Do for others what you want them to do for you. This is the teaching of the laws of Moses in a nutshell. (Matthew 7:12 LB)

Jesus Teachings of Helping The Poor
Matthew 25:31-40

- "But when I, the Messiah, shall come in my glory, and all the angels with me, then I shall sit upon my throne of glory.

- And all the nations shall be gathered before me. And I will separate the people as a shepherd separates the sheep from the goats,

- and place the sheep at my right hand, and the goats at my left.

- "Then I, the King, shall say to those at my right, 'Come, blessed of my Father, into the Kingdom prepared for you from the founding of the world.

- For I was hungry and you fed me; I was thirsty and you gave me water; I was a stranger and you invited me into your homes;

- naked and you clothed me; sick and in prison, and you visited me.'

- "Then these righteous ones will reply, 'Sir, when did we ever see you hungry and feed you? Or thirsty and give you anything to drink?

From Modern Times to Ancient Times

- Or a stranger, and help you? Or naked, and clothe you?
- When did we ever see you sick or in prison, and visit you?'
- "And I, the King, will tell them, 'When you did it to these my brothers you were doing it to me!' (Matthew 25:31-40 LB)

Loving Your Neighbor James 2:8-9

- If ye fulfill the royal law according to the scripture, Thou shalt love thy neighbor as thyself, ye do well:
- But if ye have respect to persons, ye commit sin, and are convinced of the law as transgressors. (James 2:8-9 KJV).

Mary the Teenage Mother of Jesus - Luke 1:26-38.

- The following month God sent the angel Gabriel to Nazareth, a village in Galilee,
- to a virgin, Mary, engaged to be married to a man named Joseph, a descendant of King David.
- Gabriel appeared to her and said, "Congratulations, favored lady! The Lord is with you!"
- Confused and disturbed, Mary tried to think what the angel could mean.

Teens and Young People Who Impacted the World

- "Don't be frightened, Mary," the angel told her, "for God has decided to wonderfully bless you!

- Very soon now, you will become pregnant and have a baby boy, and you are to name him 'Jesus.'

- He shall be very great and shall be called the Son of God. And the Lord God shall give him the throne of his ancestor David.

- And he shall reign over Israel forever; his Kingdom shall never end!"

- Mary asked the angel, "But how can I have a baby? I am a virgin."

- The angel replied, "The Holy Spirit shall come upon you, and the power of God shall overshadow you; so the baby born to you will be utterly holy-- the Son of God.

- Furthermore, six months ago your Aunt Elizabeth-- 'the barren one,' they called her-- became pregnant in her old age!

- For every promise from God shall surely come true."

- Mary said, "I am the Lord's servant, and I am willing to do whatever he wants. May everything you said come true." And then the angel disappeared." (Luke 1:26-38 LB)

From Modern Times to Ancient Times

Jesus's Teenage Disciples

Modern day scholars now suggest that some of Jesus's disciples or perhaps most of His Jewish disciples may have been teenagers, particularly the brothers James and John. John was the one who was often referred to as the "disciple whom Jesus loved" and the one who would lie on Jesus chest, like a child would lie on his father's chest . It was their mother who asked Jesus to let her sons sit next to Him in the Kingdom (heaven).

In Jewish tradition, a son, unlike the girl who could give herself for marriage at the age of twelve and a half, would have to wait until age eighteen. Up until that time he was subject to his parents (Luke 2:51). This may be the reason why the mother of James and John made such a request on their behalf (Matthew 20:21-22).

Scriptures regarding Young John — St John 13:21-25

- When Jesus has thus said, he was troubled in spirit, and testified and said, "Verily, verily I say unto you, that one of you shall betray me."
- Then the disciples looked one on another, doubting of whom he spake.

- Now there was **leaning on Jesus' bosom one of his disciples, whom Jesus loved**.
- Simon Peter therefore beckoned him, that he should ask who it should be of whom he spake.
- He then **lying on Jesus breast** saith unto him, Lord who is it? (St. John 13:21-25 KJV)

Scriptures Regarding The Mother's Request

- Then came to him the mother of Zebedee children with her sons, worshiping him, and desiring a certain thing.
- And he said unto her, "What will thou? She saith unto him, Grant that these my two sons may sit, the one on thy right hand and the other on the left, in thy kingdom. (Matthew 10:20-21 KJV)

Esther – The Teen Queen

She was young, wise, beautiful, courageous and obedient, and she used all of these qualities to save her people. Esther was one of several virgins competing in the Babylonian beauty contest to see who would become the next queen. It is estimated that she was only seventeen or eighteen when she was chosen to be queen.

From Modern Times to Ancient Times

A Young Virgin - Esther 2:2-9

- Then said the king's servants that ministered unto him, Let there be ***fair young*** virgins sought for the king:
- And let the king appoint officers in all the provinces of his kingdom, that they may gather together all the ***fair young virgins*** unto Shushan the palace, to the house of the women, unto the custody of Hege the king's chamberlain, keeper of the women; and let their things for purification be given them:
- And let the maiden which pleaseth the king be queen instead of Vashti. And the thing pleased the king; and he did so.
- Now in Shushan the palace there was a certain Jew, whose name was Mordecai, the son of Jair, the son of Shimei, the son of Kish, a Benjamite;
- Who had been carried away from Jerusalem with the captivity which had been carried away with Jeconiah king of Judah, whom Nebuchadnezzar the king of Babylon had carried away.
- And he brought up Hadassah, that is, Esther, his uncle's daughter: for she had neither father nor mother, and ***the maid was fair and beautiful***; whom Mordecai, when her father and mother were dead, took for his own daughter.
- So it came to pass, when the king's commandment and his decree was heard, and when many maidens

- were gathered together unto Shushan the palace, to the custody of Hegai, that Esther was brought also unto the king's house, to the custody of Hegai, keeper of the women.
- And the maiden pleased him, and she obtained kindness of him; and he speedily gave her her things for purification, with such things as belonged to her, and seven maidens, which were meet to be given her, out of the king's house: and he preferred her and her maids unto the best place of the house of the women. (Esther 2:2-9 KJV)

David - The Child Chosen to be King

While he was just a lad, he was chosen to be the second King of Israel. The little boy had not reached the age of puberty (preteen) when he was anointed and appointed to be king of Israel. He was known as a skilled musician, but his claimed to fame came when he slayed Goliath, the nine-foot giant. In Jewish history, David is considered to be Israel's greatest king, a king who developed a reputation of being "a man after God's own heart."

Young David Anointed 1 Samuel 16:6-12

- And it came to pass, when they were come, that he looked on Eliab, and said, Surely the LORD's anointed is before him.
- But the LORD said unto Samuel, Look not on his countenance, or on the height of his stature;

From Modern Times to Ancient Times

because I have refused him: for the LORD seeth not as man seeth; for man looketh on the outward appearance, but the LORD looketh on the heart.

- Then Jesse called Abinadab, and made him pass before Samuel. And he said, Neither hath the LORD chosen this.

- Then Jesse made Shammah to pass by. And he said, Neither hath the LORD chosen this.

- Again, Jesse made seven of his sons to pass before Samuel. And Samuel said unto Jesse, The LORD hath not chosen these.

- And Samuel said unto Jesse, Are here all thy *children*? And he said, There remaineth yet the *youngest*, and, behold, he keepeth the sheep. And Samuel said unto Jesse, Send and fetch him: for we will not sit down till he come hither.

- And he sent, and brought him in. Now he was ruddy, and withal of a beautiful countenance, and goodly to look to. And the LORD said, *Arise, anoint him*: for this is he.

- Then Samuel took the horn of oil, and anointed him in the midst of his brethren: and the Spirit of the LORD came upon David from that day forward. So Samuel rose up, and went to Ramah. (I Samuel 16:6-12 KJV)

Young David Prepared To Fight Goliath

- And Saul armed David with his armour, and he put an helmet of brass upon his head; also he armed him with a coat of mail.

- And when the Philistine looked about, and saw David, he disdained him, for he was but a youth, and ruddy and of fair countenance. (I Samuel 17:39 & 42 KJV)

Solomon – The Teenage King of Wisdom

Known for his wisdom and for deciding the case between two women who were claiming custody of the same baby, Solomon was chosen to be King of Israel at the age of twelve. Although Solomon is known for being one of the wisest men on earth, seldom has he been known as the "teenager" who succeeded his father, King David.

The Wise Teenage King - I Kings 3:7-14

- And now, O LORD my God, thou hast made thy servant king instead of David my father: and I am but a little child: I know not how to go out or come in.

- And thy servant is in the midst of thy people which thou hast chosen, a great people, that cannot be numbered nor counted for multitude.

From Modern Times to Ancient Times

- Give therefore thy servant an understanding heart to judge thy people, that I may discern between good and bad: for who is able to judge this thy so great a people?

- And the speech pleased the Lord, that Solomon had asked this thing.

- And God said unto him, Because thou hast asked this thing, and hast not asked for thyself long life; neither hast asked riches for thyself, nor hast asked the life of thine enemies; but hast asked for thyself understanding to discern judgment;

- Behold, I have done according to thy words: lo, I have given thee a wise and an understanding heart; so that there was none like thee before thee, neither after thee shall any arise like unto thee.

- And I have also given thee that which thou hast not asked, both riches, and honour: so that there shall not be any among the kings like unto thee all thy days.

- And if thou wilt walk in my ways, to keep my statutes and my commandments, as thy father David did walk, then I will lengthen thy days. (I Kings 3:7-14 KJV)

Samuel - The Child Priest

He was barely five years old when he started his priesthood training, he went on to become one of Israel's greatest priests.

The Child Priest - I Samuel 2:18-21 & 26

- But Samuel ministered before the LORD, being a child, girded with a linen ephod.

- Moreover his mother made him a little coat, and brought it to him from year to year, when she came up with her husband to offer the yearly sacrifice.

- And Eli blessed Elkanah and his wife, and said, The LORD give thee seed of this woman for the loan which is lent to the LORD. And they went unto their own home.

- And the LORD visited Hannah, so that she conceived, and bare three sons and two daughters. And the child Samuel grew before the LORD.

- And the child Samuel grew on, and was in favour both with the LORD, and also with men. (I Samuel 2:18-21 &26 KJV)

Little Samuel Answers The Call – I Samuel 3:1-10

- And the child Samuel ministered unto the LORD before Eli. And the word of the LORD was precious in those days; there was no open vision.

From Modern Times to Ancient Times

- And it came to pass at that time, when Eli was laid down in his place, and his eyes began to wax dim, that he could not see;

- And ere the lamp of God went out in the temple of the LORD, where the ark of God was, and Samuel was laid down to sleep;

- That the LORD called Samuel: and he answered, Here am I.

- And he ran unto Eli, and said, Here am I; for thou calledst me. And he said, I called not; lie down again. And he went and lay down.

- And the LORD called yet again, Samuel. And Samuel arose and went to Eli, and said, Here am I; for thou didst call me. And he answered, I called not, my son; lie down again.

- Now Samuel did not yet know the LORD, neither was the word of the LORD yet revealed unto him.

- And the LORD called Samuel again the third time. And he arose and went to Eli, and said, Here am I; for thou didst call me. And Eli perceived that the LORD had called the child.

- Therefore Eli said unto Samuel, Go, lie down: and it shall be, if he call thee, that thou shalt say, Speak, LORD; for thy servant heareth. So Samuel went and lay down in his place.

- And the LORD came, and stood, and called as at other times, Samuel, Samuel. Then Samuel answered, Speak; for thy servant heareth. (I Samuel 3:1-10 KJV)

Josiah - The Godly Child King

Of all the kings in the Bible, young Josiah was one of the few kings that pleased God. In fact, he cleaned up the ungodly mess that the other older kings had left behind.

The Eight Year Old King - 2 Chronicles 34:1-3

- Josiah was eight years old when he began to reign, and he reigned in Jerusalem one and thirty years.
- And he did that which was right in the sight of the LORD, and walked in the ways of David his father, and declined neither to the right hand, nor to the left.
- For in the eighth year of his reign, while he was yet young, he began to seek after the God of David his father: and in the twelfth year he began to purge Judah and Jerusalem from the high places, and the groves, and the carved images, and the molten images. (2 Chronicles 34:1-3 KJV)

Daniel & His Friends– The Teenage Heroes

The Story of Daniel in the lion's den and the story of Shadrach, Meshach and Abednego in the fiery furnace, are two of the most popular Sunday School stories in the Bible for both children and adults. But very few Sunday school teachers acknowledge that Daniel and his three courageous friends were only teenagers. The scriptures refer to them being children, children with no blemish, meaning teenager with no pimples.

All four teenagers were courageous and refused to compromise in a very hostile environment. As a result of their courageous stand, they gained favor during their captivity and were appointed to high political positions. The following scriptures refer to their youth.

Daniel & the Teenage Heroes – Daniel 1:3-7

- And the king spake unto Ashpenaz the master of his eunuchs, that he should bring certain of the children of Israel, and of the king's seed, and of the princes;

- Children in whom was no blemish, but well favoured, and skillful in all wisdom, and cunning in knowledge, and understanding science, and such as had ability in them to stand in the king's palace, and whom they might teach the learning and the tongue of the Chaldeans.

- And the king appointed them a daily provision of the king's meat, and of the wine which he drank: so nourishing them three years, that at the end thereof they might stand before the king.

- Now among these were of the children of Judah, Daniel, Hananiah, Mishael, and Azariah:

- Unto whom the prince of the eunuchs gave names: for he gave unto Daniel the name of Belteshazzar; and to Hananiah, of Shadrach; and to Mishael, of Meshach; and to Azariah, of Abednego. (Daniel 1:3-7, see also Daniel 3rd and 6th Chapters).

Jeremiah – Chosen before Birth and, Ordained at Birth

Before he was born, he was chosen to be one of God's a major prophets. Jeremiah, the prophet that is known for being placed in dungeon and left to die, is seldom known for being chosen before birth.

Jeremiah Chosen – Jeremiah 1-4-10

- Then the word of the LORD came unto me, saying,
- Before I formed thee in the belly I knew thee; and before thou camest forth out of the womb I sanctified thee, and I ordained thee a prophet unto the nations.
- Then said I, Ah, Lord GOD! behold, I cannot speak: for I am a child.
- But the LORD said unto me, Say not, I am a child: for thou shalt go to all that I shall send thee, and whatsoever I command thee thou shalt speak.
- Be not afraid of their faces: for I am with thee to deliver thee, saith the LORD.

- Then the LORD put forth his hand, and touched my mouth. And the LORD said unto me, Behold, I have put my words in thy mouth.
- See, I have this day set thee over the nations and over the kingdoms, to root out, and to pull down, and to destroy, and to throw down, to build, and to plant. (Jeremiah 1:4-10 KJV)

Joseph – A Teenager with Foresight

Joseph was not only an extraordinary child who would use his foresight to become the second most powerful man in Egypt. What is amazing, is that he, like many other great men and women, started demonstrating his unique ability as a teenager.

Teenager With Foresight - Genesis 37:2-5

- These are the generations of Jacob. Joseph, being seventeen years old, was feeding the flock with his brethren; and the lad was with the sons of Bilhah, and with the sons of Zilpah, his father's wives: and Joseph brought unto his father their evil report.
- Now Israel loved Joseph more than all his children, because he was the son of his old age: and he made him a coat of many colors.
- And when his brethren saw that their father loved him more than all his brethren, they hated him, and could not speak peaceably unto him.

- And Joseph dreamed a dream, and he told it his brethren: and they hated him yet the more. (Genesis 37:2-5 KJV).

Adam and Eve –In Their Late Teens?

One of the first assignments given by God to the couple in the Garden of Eden was to "have dominion" over his creation and "replenish the earth." It is believed by most scholars that the first couple was more likely to have been young, strong, and in their prime. In most cases, this would mean that they were probably in their mid to late teens or early twenties. The fact that they were inquisitive regarding the fruit on the forbidden tree, may also be evidence of their youthfulness and immaturity.

Young Adam and Eve – Genesis 1-27-30

- So God created man in his own image, in the image of God created he him; male and female created he them.

- And God blessed them, and God said unto them, Be fruitful, and multiply, and replenish the earth, and subdue it: and have dominion over the fish of the sea, and over the fowl of the air, and over every living thing that moveth upon the earth.

- And God said, Behold, I have given you every herb bearing seed, which is upon the face of all the earth, and every tree, in the which is the fruit of a tree yielding seed; to you it shall be for meat.

- And to every beast of the earth, and to every fowl of the air, and to every thing that creepeth upon the earth, wherein there is life, I have given every green herb for meat: and it was so. (Genesis 1:27-30 KJV)

St. Paul's Advice To Teenagers & Young People

- Let no man despise thy youth; but be thou an example of the believers, in word, in conversation, in love in spirit, in faith, in purity.
- Till I come, give attendance to reading, to exhortation, to doctrine.
- Neglect not the gift that is in thee… (I Timothy 4:11-14 NKJV)

Bibliography

Louis Jacobs, *The Jewish Religion: A Companion*: New York, Oxford University Press, 1995

Anita Diamant and Howard Cooper, *Living A Jewish Life: Jewish Traditions, Customs and Values for Today's Families*: New York, Harper Collins Publishers, 1991

Dr. Cecil Roth & Dr. Geoffrey Wigoder, *The New Standard Jewish Encyclopedia*, New York, Doubleday & Company, 1970

William Whiston, *Josephus: The Complete Works*, Thomas Nelson Publishers, Nashville, Tennessee, 1998

Ronald F. Youngblood, E.F. Bruce & R.K. Harrison, *New Bible Dictionary*, Nashville, Tennessee, 1995

James M. Washington & Coretta Scott King, *Martin Luther King: I Have A Dream: Writing & Speeches*, New York, Harper Collins Publishers, 1992

Harris Wofford, *Of Kennedys & Kings: Making Sense of the Sixties*, Toronto Canada, McGraw Hill, 1980

Ann S. Manheimer, *Martin Luther King Jr.: Dreaming of Equality*, Minneapolis, MN, Corolrhoda Books Inc., 2005

Teens and Young People Who Impacted the World

Taylor Branch, *At Canaan's Edge: America in the King Years 1965-1968*: New York, Simon & Schuster, 2006

Dr. Bernard Schwartz, *Statutory History of the United States Civil Rights Part I & Part II*, New York, McGraw Hill, 1970

Julie Witcover, Party of the People: A History of the Democrats, Random House Inc. New York, 2003

Harry A. Ploski & James Williams, The Negro Almanac: A Reference Work on the African American, Detroit MI, Gale Research Inc., 1989

Darlene Clark Hine, *Black Women In America; An Historical Encyclopedia*, Brooklyn New York, Carlson Publishing Inc., 1993

Kenneth C. Davis, *Rosa Parks*, New York, Harpers Collins Publishers, 2005

Rackham Holt, *George Washington Carver: An American Biography*, Garden City, New York, Doubleday Publishers, 1944

William J. Federer, *George Washington Carver: His Life and Faith in his Own Words*, St Louis MO, Amerisearch Inc., 2002

William J. Federer, *America's God and Country: Encyclopedia of Quotations*, St Louis MO, FAME Publishers 1994

Shannon Zemlicka, *Thomas Edison*, Minneapolis, MN, Lerner Publications Company, 2004

From Modern Times to Ancient Times

Cynthia Klingel and Robert B. Noyed, *Thomas Edison: Inventor*, Chanhassen, MN, The Child's World, 2003

Frieda Wishinsky, *Albert Einstein: A Photographic Story of a Life*, New York, D.K. Publishing, 2005

Diane Stanley, *Leonardo Da Vinci*, New York, William Morrow & Company Inc., 1996

Marc Davis, *Florence Nightingale: Founder of the Nightingale School of Nursing*, Chanhassen, MN, The Child's World, 2004

Helen S. Garson, *Oprah Winfrey: A Biography*, Westport CT, Greenwood Press, 2004

Geraldine Woods, *The Oprah Winfrey Story: Speaking Her Mind*, Minneapolis, MN, Dillion Press, Inc., 1991

Tanya Lee Stone, *Oprah Winfrey: Success With An Open Heart*, Brookfield, Connecticut, Millbrook Press, 2001

Craig Peters, *Bill Gates: Software Genius of Microsoft*, Russell, Massachusetts, Chestnut Productions & Enslow Publishers Inc., 2003

Stewart Ross, *Wolfgang Amadeus Mozart: Musical Genius*, Chicago, IL, Raintree Publishers, 2004

Roland Vernon, *Introducing Mozart*, Parsippany, NJ, Silver Burdett Press, 1996

Julie Downing, *Mozart Tonight*, New York, Macmillan Publishing Company, New York, 1991

Teens and Young People Who Impacted the World

Meg Green, *Mother Teresa: A Biography*, Westport, CT, Greenwood Press, 2004

Nina Morgan, *Mother Teresa: Saint of the Poor*, Austin, TX, Steck-Vaughn Company, 1998

Resources also include: Encyclopedia Britannica 1992 Edition, internet research. King James and Living versions of the Bible, and documentaries by A&E Network and History Channel.

Photos

http://en.wikipedia.org/wiki/Oprah_Winfrey

http://en.wikipedia.org/wiki/File:Rosaparks.jpg

http://en.wikipedia.org/wiki/Albert_Einstein

http://en.wikipedia.org/wiki/File:Selma_to_Montgomery_Marches.jpg

http://en.wikipedia.org/wiki/Florence_Nightingale

http://en.wikipedia.org/wiki/Thomas_Edison

http://en.wikipedia.org/wiki/Mother_Teresa

http://en.wikipedia.org/wiki/George_Washington_Carver

http://en.wikipedia.org/wiki/Wolfgang_Amadeus_Mozart

http://en.wikipedia.org/wiki/Leonardo_da_Vinci

Christmas baby © Photowitch | Dreamstime.com

Portrait of Jesus in prayer © Carlosphotos | Dreamstime.com

Bible series esther © Stephen Orsillo | Dreamstime.com